W9-AYQ-917

Troy

LOST WORLDS AND MYSTERIOUS CIVILIZATIONS

Atlantis

Easter Island

El Dorado

The Maya

Nubia

Pompeii

Roanoke

Troy

LOST WORLDS AND MYSTERIOUS CIVILIZATIONS

Troy

Samuel Willard Crompton

CHELSEA HOUSE
An Infobase Learning Company

Troy

Copyright ©2012 by Infobase Learning

Chelsea House
An imprint of Infobase Learning
132 West 31st Street
New York, NY 10001

Library of Congress Cataloging-in-Publication Data
Crompton, Samuel Willard.
  Troy / by Samuel Willard Crompton.
      p. cm. — (Lost worlds and mysterious civilizations)
  Includes bibliographical references and index.
  ISBN 978-1-60413-974-7 (hardcover)
  1. Troy (Extinct city)—Juvenile literature. I. Title.
  DF221.T8C76 2011
  939'.21—dc22   2011011618

Chelsea House books are available at special discounts when purchased in bulk quantities for businesses, associations, institutions, or sales promotions. Please call our Special Sales Department in New York at (212) 967-8800 or (800) 322-8755.

You can find Chelsea House on the World Wide Web at http://www.infobaselearning.com

Text design by Erika K. Arroyo
Cover design by Alicia Post
Composition by EJB Publishing Services
Cover printed by Yurchak Printing, Landisville, Pa.
Book printed and bound by Yurchak Printing, Landisville, Pa.
Date printed: December 2011
Printed in the United States of America

10 9 8 7 6 5 4 3 2 1

This book is printed on acid-free paper.

Contents

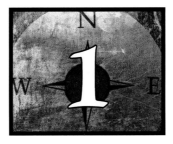

The Royal Diadem

Was Helen blonde or brunette?

Did Greece send 1,000 ships to bring her back?

Could the wooden horse really have been the instrument of Troy's destruction?

These questions and others—ranging from the trivial to the sublime—have been posed by dozens of succeeding generations, each inspired in turn by the words of the *Iliad* and the *Odyssey*.

THE SOURCE

In many historical situations, the reader—or listener—has a variety of sources from which to draw, and one of his or her tasks is to separate the likely from the impossible. This is not the case with Troy and the Trojan War, however; our one great source is sometimes our *only* source. At least 90 percent of everything we know about Troy in the Late Bronze Age comes from the inspired lips of Homer, an eighth-century-B.C. Greek poet.

Lips and *listeners* are significant words because Homer—to the best of our knowledge—never wrote anything. Homer traveled what is now western Turkey, singing two great epic tales that were later carved into blocks of stone or clay, and even later put onto papyrus and manuscript. The *Iliad* and the *Odyssey* are Homer's works, but they come to us moderns over the distance of 2,800 years and numerous translations.

Though we are confident Homer existed—and that he was the great poet who gave the *Iliad* and the *Odyssey* their distinctive shape—much about him remains obscure. Historians believe that Homer lived in the eighth century before Christ, about 400 years after the events of the Trojan War, and that he sang about a time that he considered grander, more glorious than his own. But was he blind, as some of the stories have it? And if so, how could he have visualized the great plain of Troy? Did he sing to goatherds and shepherds in local taverns, or did he entertain kings and aristocrats? Finally, perhaps most importantly, did he travel to the various sites he describes in his beautiful poetry, or was it all the figment of an amazing imaginative power?

Since Homer sang, 2,800 years have passed, and it is possible that some of these questions will never be answered. There are others that have been addressed, however, and in the early twenty-first century we know more about Troy, the Trojans, and the invading Greeks than ever before. Part of what we will lay out in this work is the combination of literary and archaeological evidence, the twists and turns of Homer's writing, and the shovels and spades used by four generations of scientists who have stood on the ruins of Troy. Almost every one of them has kept the *Iliad* and the *Odyssey* close at hand as they dug.

We will commence with Homer, picking up the action in Book III of the *Iliad*.

THE CHALLENGE

Book III begins with Prince Hector and Prince Paris, brothers, issuing a challenge to the Greeks. Everyone knows that the nine-year-long war was caused by the abduction of Helen, formerly queen of Sparta. She has been at Troy for nine years, as the wife of Paris, and the Greeks have come across the Aegean Sea to reclaim her and despoil Troy at the same time. Nine years have left their mark on the city and its people. Thousands of good men have bled and died on the wheat fields and open plain before Troy. Rather than let any more perish, Paris issues his challenge to Menelaus, the king of Sparta and Helen's former husband.

The two men will fight a duel on the open ground, in full view of the two armies. If the Spartan, Menelaus, prevails, then Helen and the treasure she brought with her shall return to Sparta. If the Trojan, Paris, wins,

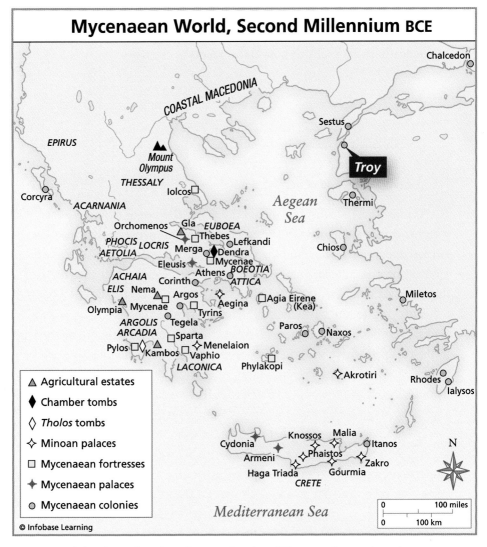

Mycenaean World, Second Millennium BCE

Chalcedon

COASTAL MACEDONIA

Sestus

EPIRUS

Mount Olympus

THESSALY

Iolcos

Corcyra

ACARNANIA

Troy

Aegean Sea

Thermi

Orchomenos Gla EUBOEA

PHOCIS LOCRIS Thebes Lefkandi

AETOLIA Merga Dendra

Chios

Eleusis Mycenae

ACHAIA Athens BOEOTIA

Corinth ATTICA

ELIS Nema

Argos

Olympia Mycenae Aegina Agia Eirene (Kea)

ARGOLIS Tyrins

ARCADIA Tegela

Sparta Paros

Pylos Kambos Menelaion Naxos

Vaphio

LACONICA Phylakopi

Miletos

Akrotiri

Rhodes

Ialysos

Agricultural estates

Chamber tombs

Tholos tombs

Minoan palaces

Mycenaean fortresses

Mycenaean palaces

Mycenaean colonies

Knossos Malia

Cydonia

Armeni Phaistos Itanos

Haga Triada Gournia Zakro

CRETE

N

Mediterranean Sea

0		100 miles
0		100 km

© Infobase Learning

Around the time of ancient Greece, the city of Troy was located on the western coast of Turkey. It is believed that Homer, the poet who wrote about Troy and the Trojan War in his epic the *Iliad*, had traveled throughout the region.

then the Greeks shall strike their tents and embark on their ships, never to trouble Troy again.

We imagine the common soldier, on either side, elated by the idea. Let the great champions fight and allow the common man to be done with this nine-year contest. The nobles also agree, and as the two sides debate as to how the duel shall be conducted, the scene shifts to inside the city, where Helen learns that her former husband and her present one will soon fight to the death. Homer tells us how Helen reacts to the news:

> And with those words
> the goddess [Aphrodite] filled her heart with yearning warm and deep
> for her husband long ago, her city and her parents.
> Quickly cloaking herself in shimmering linen,
> out of her rooms she rushed, live tears welling,
> and not alone—two of her women followed close behind.

The last sentence displays one of the major themes of Homer's poetry: whether one is alone or with friends at crucial moments in life's journey. All too often, in the *Iliad* and the *Odyssey*, one finds that one's friends are far away or unavailable. That is not the case with Helen on this particular day, however.

Hurrying to the battlements, Helen arrives at the "looming Scaean Gates," another of the set pieces Homer uses time and again. On her way to the parapet, where she will enjoy a good view of the duel, Helen passes by a number of leading Trojan military men, fellows who have the equivalent of what we today would call a chest full of medals. They view her with a mixture of amazement and disdain. "Beauty, terrible beauty!" they say.

Helen knows very well what the Trojans think of her. Ever since arriving in their fair city nine years earlier, she has received a mixture of pity, anger, contempt, and admiration. She knows all too well the effect of her beauty on men, and she has long grown accustomed to the envy it produces among women. Passing by the Trojan generals, Helen is about to see the action, when she hears a friendly voice:

> Come over here, dear child. Sit in front of me,
> so you can see your husband of long ago,
> your kinsmen and your people.
> I don't blame you. I hold the gods to blame.
> They are the ones who brought this war upon me,
> devastating war against the Achaeans.

It is none other than King Priam, the father of Hector and Paris, and therefore Helen's father-in-law. He is pictured by Homer—throughout the *Iliad*—as a venerable man, wise with the passage of years, and sorrowful over what is happening to his city. Had Priam sent Helen back to the Greeks nine years earlier, the war might not have taken place, but he has long since steeled himself to the rigors of this conflict. Whether he will prevail in the end or fall to the enemy's sword, Priam will be Priam: elderly, beneficent, noble.

The king goes on to ask Helen about some of the Greek leaders he sees in the distance. The view from the parapet over the Scaean Gates is high above the plain, and Helen can make out the distinctive clothing and armor of her former countrymen. She replies:

> I revere you so, dear father, dread you too—
> if only death had pleased me then, grim death,
> that day I followed your son to Troy, forsaking
> my marriage bed, my kinsmen and my child,
> my favorite, now full-grown,
> and the lovely comradeship of women my own age.

Helen speaks the words of the exile, a condition known to many men and women of the Bronze Age (we will say more about the "lovely comradeship" later). But she answers Priam's question:

> I have the answer.
> That man is Atreus' son Agamemnon, lord of empires,
> Both a mighty king and a strong spearman too,
> And he used to be my kinsman, whore that I am!
> There was a world . . . or was it all a dream?

Both Helen and the reader pause here, for what man or woman has not sometimes felt like a failure, and what person—man, woman, or child—does not occasionally wonder if what they experience is a dream? King Priam continues to point out other Greek champions, however, and Helen must name and describe them:

> That's Laertes' son, the great tactician Odysseus.
> He was bred in the land of Ithaca. Rocky ground
> and he's quick at every treachery under the sun—
> the man of twists and turns.

Odysseus will, of course, play a leading role in the events that follow, but one cannot quite discern—from Helen's tone of voice—whether his skill at treachery is admired, loathed, or feared. Priam points to another Greek, one of the largest of them all, and Helen replies:

> Why, that's the giant Ajax, bulwark of the Achaeans.
> And Idomeneus over there—standing with his Cretans—
> Like a god, you see? And the Cretan captains
> Form a ring around him. How often Menelaus,
> My good soldier, would host him in our halls,
> In the old days, when he'd sail across from Crete.

Homer is so skillful a narrator that we—the readers or listeners—cannot be certain whether he throws Crete and its people in merely for color, or to demonstrate the close tie between mainland Greece and the island of Crete. Twentieth-century archaeology would bring a greater knowledge of that situation.

Helen does not have time to identify any more Greek champions (Homer often calls them the Achaeans or the Argives) because Priam is called to leave the city. He goes out in his chariot car (as they were called) to be present at the duel between his son and the Spartan king.

THE DUEL

Fights between champions appear to have been common in the Bronze Age. Military technology—ranging from boar's tusk helmets to bronze daggers inlaid with gold—had progressed to the point where it was more efficient to have the leaders fight (so long as there were commoners available to groom their horses and polish their armor). Though we cannot be certain this precise duel took place (we have no corroborative source), it is likely that such challenges did occur in the fighting between Greeks and Trojans.

Paris of Troy and Menelaus of Sparta meet on the open ground between the two armies. The Trojan—at least in our modern-day minds—is the handsomer, more athletic person, while the Spartan is older, heavier, and much more experienced in hand-to-hand combat. As Homer describes it, Menelaus uses his spear and shield to great effect, battering Paris unmercifully, and, just at the moment when it appears that all is lost, the goddess Aphrodite intervenes. She frees Paris from Menelaus' grip and lifts him to safety, on the other side of Troy's great walls. As Homer describes it, neither the Greeks nor the Trojans can be certain whether this is an act of the gods or a magician's trick, but in either case the truce has been broken. The two

According to the *Iliad*, the Trojan War began when Helen, the queen of Sparta, left her husband for Paris, the prince of Troy. Menelaus, the fierce king of Sparta, assembled his allies to take back his wife and exact revenge on Paris. Above, a relief of Menelaus and Helen from the sixth century B.C.

armies surge to meet each other on the open field, and the scene shifts to the walls of Troy, where Helen and Paris are reunited.

We modern readers do not have to accept Homer's view of gods and goddesses intervening in the affairs of men and women. What is important is to realize that the Greeks of Homer's time—and their ancestors, 400 years earlier—*did* see the world as a strange combination of earthly and heavenly, with the wills and desires of human beings often thwarted by those of the gods.

Let us leave Homer at this point, in the middle of Book III of the *Iliad*. Let us go forward 2,800 years.

ROYAL DIADEM

In the winter of 1994–1995, 3,200 years after the events of the Trojan War, historians and archaeologists were astonished to learn that Trojan treasures were on display in a Russian museum in St. Petersburg. These particular treasures (collectively known as "King Priam's Treasures") had been missing for many years, and some scholars had begun to doubt their very existence. Through a series of strange events, they ended up in Russia, and the specialists that were allowed to see them in 1995 confirmed that what they saw was what they had hoped for. The treasures of Troy—whether they were Priam's or someone else's—were substantially intact. A book cataloguing the entire exhibit has this to say about the larger of the two diadems (crowns):

> *From a thin, horizontal chain hang 90 single, vertical chains decorated with gold plates in the shape of slightly convex leaves with a pronounced vertical central rib. The plates are strung on to the chains every two links through a hole in the upper parts of the plate. The short central chains have between 27 and 29 plates; long ones at the side have 106–110 plates. Sixteen chains at the sides—eight on the left and eight on the right—frame a row of 74 central shorter chains decorated with pendants in the shape of a double lead or lance shapes, each of which has a long vertical rib. On the reverse of the diadem, about half way down, all the vertical chains are linked together by a horizontal gold chain, and the long chains at the sides are further secured with three gold plates.*

It seems incredible that such beauty—and riches—could come from the Bronze Age. Only the Romans, in the time of Julius Caesar, had been known to possess such wealth. But the people that attended the Moscow exhibit in 1995 found that the objects answered to the description, and most accepted the idea that these treasures came from Priam's Troy. Because it was a diadem, meant for the forehead of a king or queen, Americans, Russians, and others naturally posed a handful of questions.

Did this masterpiece of gold on gold belong to King Priam?

Did it ever grace his brow?

Was it ever, perhaps, lent to Helen, so that she might show off the gold and glory of her adopted city?

Questions such as these, over the provenance of objects of art, often lead the reader to a series of other ones, based more in the nature of philosophy and speculation.

Was Troy really so rich?

Did the Greeks come for Helen, or for plunder?

And, last but not least, what can the Trojan War tell us about the peoples of the Bronze Age, and, by extension, of ourselves?

Lay of the Land,
Tug of the Water

Many things change in a lifetime, or series of them, but the lands and waters around Troy are substantially the same as they were in Homer's time, and that of Priam's as well. By becoming familiar with the goat paths and ship crossings of the Bronze Age, we will come to understand why Troy and its people were natural rivals of the Greeks. We will see why a mighty fleet—whether of 1,000 ships or not—sailed across the Aegean to besiege Troy.

COMING BY LAND

Let us imagine a group of merchant-travelers, departing the ancient city of Babylon about 1300 B.C. Babylon, in present-day Iraq, was one of the great powers of the Middle East, one whose rulers used the term *Great King* in letters to other monarchs. These merchants are less interested in power politics than in making a living, and, given that this was the Bronze Age—a time when nobles adorned themselves with all sorts of accoutrements (superficial accessories)—let us conjecture that they are bringing oil, spices, and carpets for sale.

Babylon has been a trading metropolis for almost 2,000 years, and its people know the roads and currents as well as anyone. Let us follow the merchant-travelers as they leave Mesopotamia ("The Land Between the Rivers") on their way to Troy.

Departing Babylon, our merchants progress along the west bank of the Euphrates River, headed north by northwest. Their first few nights are spent in Babylonian territory, where the greatest difficulty lies in finding the best inn, but within a week they are in Assyria, an up-and-coming power that is beginning to rival Babylon in size and prestige. There is peace, currently, between Babylon and Assyria, and the merchant-travelers are given a cordial—though not hearty—welcome. The Assyrians have access to the same markets as Babylon, and they are not keen on allowing foreign merchants to take profits that might belong to their own nationals.

After 10 or perhaps 12 days in Assyria, the merchants cross the line into what is now Turkey and was then called Anatolia. Within three days, they enter the land of the Hittites, another of the major players in Middle Eastern power politics of the Bronze Age.

Less is known—then and today—of the Hittites than the Babylonians or the Assyrians. The Hittites were masters at keeping things secret, and the merchant-travelers are able to learn little about the military or diplomatic activities of the Hittite Empire. What they do see, and what undoubtedly creates a strong impression, is the size of the major Hittite cities in eastern and central Turkey. Not only are these cities well walled and guarded, but there are impressive sculptures of a set of gods and goddesses different from those worshipped in Babylon, Assyria, or Greece, for that matter. The "Storm god" seems to be the highest, most important of the Hittite pantheon.

Crossing the Hittite Empire takes our travelers a solid six weeks. There are rural areas, where the people seem much like any others, and urban centers, where the Hittite influence seems different from anything that has come before. Let us conjecture that our merchant-travelers—men good at striking up conversations—ask about the lands to the west and are especially interested in the place called Wilusa.

It is one of the allies of the Hittite Empire, the answer comes, and is important for the number of trade goods that pass through its walls. The people are not Hittites; they are of a different ethnic group, but for decades they have been allies and friends. The people of Wilusa, which modern scholars believe is synonymous with Troy, are also excellent horse breeders, and the Hittite leaders often purchase stallions and mares from that city. Continuing the journey, the merchants depart the Hittite Empire and venture into the lesser-known areas to the west. Most, if not all, these peoples are friends and allies of the Hittites, but given that the entire Middle East is in a period of political instability, one cannot be certain from one year to the next.

Finally, after weeks of meandering through the river valleys and high plains of Turkey, the merchants come within sight of Wilusa (Troy).

The city straddles a promontory overlooking the Turkish plain, and the wind cuts through the area constantly, causing shivers up the spine and a certain sense of anxiety. Nevertheless, the travelers marvel at the beauty of the location; the leaders of Troy have clearly made some wise decisions.

Coming from the southeast, the merchants see more of the city as they progress, but they are frustrated from seeing the whole because of the excellent walls. The king and his subjects have built a series of walls to guard the city, and though Troy is currently at peace, there is always the possibility of another conflict. Troy and its people have grown rich through cattle, horses, and trade, but their wealth has caused a growing envy among their neighbors. A city is only as strong as its walls, and the hearts of the people who defend them.

Whether they knock at the gates or sound a horn to announce their arrival, the merchants are questioned, examined, and perhaps even searched. When it is ascertained that they come in peace, with many trade goods, they are allowed into the beautiful city. The inns of Troy are not as sumptuous as those of Babylon, and the city is not as large as the Hittite capitals, but the travelers are pleased. This is the most civilized place they have seen for weeks, and it is pleasant simply to bathe one's feet after the long journey. On the morning of their third day, the merchants are summoned to the king.

Up and up they go, their feet aching at times, and finally they arrive at the citadel, the pinnacle of Troy. Here they find a palace and the apartments of the royal family.

The king and his relatives wish to be the first to see the wares, and while the merchants lay them out on the floor, some steal looks at the palace and the surrounding area. The king and his family have by far the best views to be found, and the merchants, who are more familiar with the low-lying cities of Mesopotamia, are stunned by the variety of land and water surrounding Troy.

Standing at the top of the citadel, one can see perhaps 50 miles to the north, and almost twice that far to the west. The central Turkish plateau blocks some of the eastward view, but looking toward the direction of the sunset, one can make out a handful of islands and—on a truly fine day—some snowcapped mountains in northern Greece, clear on the other side of the Aegean. Gazing straight north one sees the Strait of the Dardanelles, one of the world's most important strategic waterways (then and today). The Peninsula of Gallipoli—which later saw some of the most vicious fighting of the First World War—is clearly visible. The travelers are struck by the majesty of the surroundings, but they also notice the wind. It seems to blow constantly, kicking sand from the Aegean beaches onto the Turkish plain. And then—perhaps in a flash of insight—the merchants understand why Troy has grown so rich.

The prevailing winds blow from the northeast (perhaps why the Hittites venerated the Storm god), making it nearly impossible for ships to pass by Troy. Whether Greek, Phoenician, or Egyptian, ships had to pause in the natural harbor near Troy, sometimes to wait as long as two weeks for a favorable wind. During that time, they are helpless before the demands of the Trojan king and his agents: Whatever tolls Troy levies will be collected.

Troy has grown rich through a combination of land power (cattle, horses, and chariots) and its veto power over the ships of maritime nations. While other cities of the ancient world might be richer, or more powerful, Troy stands in a rather special place, where it can command the resources of the land *and* of the sea.

When they come home to Babylon, the merchants have much to say. The Hittite Empire is powerful, they say, but it does not seem to have designs on Babylon. The Assyrians are always dangerous; it is fortunate that this is a time of peace. As for Troy, the place that some people call Wilusa, it is something from a fairy tale, both blessed and cursed by its connection to the sea.

SAILING THE "WINE-DARK SEA"

Mainland Greece plays the largest role in the story of Bronze Age Troy, but, given the importance of Crete—and its people—let us imagine a ship full of merchant-travelers departing that island, sometime about 1300 B.C. Whether they considered themselves Greek, Cretan, or Minoan is difficult to say, but in each and every case, they would be an island people affiliated with the Greek mainland.

Departing the north side of Crete, our merchant adventurers would enter the Aegean, which Homer calls the "wine-dark sea." Very likely,

Although Troy traded and dealt mostly with mainland Greece, people from other islands and civilizations often visited for economic and political purposes. The Minoans (*above*) living on the modern-day island of Crete frequently sailed across the Aegean Sea to do business in Troy.

Homer was referring to the color of the water, but in an odd coincidence, some of the best archaeological finds of the twentieth and twenty-first centuries have been of wine casks, some buried with shipwrecks for 3,000 years! Certainly, the ancient Greeks—and Trojans, too—liked wine; it was one of the major commercial exports of the region.

Sailing north by northeast, our merchant-travelers soon pass by the island of Thera, known—then and today—for its volcanic cone. The volcano had exploded with great force a few centuries earlier, sending a tidal wave of water that may have destroyed an earlier phase of civilization on Crete. Whether our merchant-travelers know this, or whether they merely see Thera as another of the charming Greek islands is hard to say.

Passing Thera, our merchant group sails in and among the numerous islands of the Aegean. Many of them have storied names today, and these waters now team with cruise ships. Business would be on the minds of our travelers, though, and as their ship pulls up the Aegean into Turkish waters, they would be on the lookout for Troy, the best-known city in those parts. From the decks of their galley, the merchants would have a view complementary to what was seen by the merchants of Babylon: In this case, they would be gazing east, in the direction of the rising sun.

Troy is only a mile and a half inland, and the morning light striking its towers and walls would present a fine sight. Our merchants would know that—barring an unusual wind—they would have to anchor in the Troad (Troy's natural harbor) and pay some sort of toll to its king. Whether the merchants would disembark and spend time at Troy is uncertain. Very likely, they would be keener on selling their wares—including Greek wine and pottery—to other peoples who would pay more for them. But there was at least some trade between mainland Greece and Troy. Even if they do not go ashore, the merchants can see the islands of the Aegean, and it is apparent to them that Troy has a commanding position in the area.

WILL IT LAST?

Finally the wind shifts, allowing our merchant sailors to enter the Dardanelles. This narrow strait, only a mile wide in some sections, is the natural separation between Europe and Asia. Travelers have passed through its waters for millennia, understanding its strategic importance. Our merchant sailors, however, are keenest on seeing the back of Troy, and it is about seven miles up the Dardanelles that the Trojan city disappears from view. Our travelers then enter the Sea of Marmara.

Whether it was formed by the Great Flood or not, the Sea of Marmara is a rather strange body of water, 140 miles long and 40 miles wide. It displaces a great deal of water, but it has no visible tidal current and is a mixture of salt and fresh water. Our merchants sail easily across the Marmara; its winds are gentle compared to those of the Aegean. Only toward the north end, where the Marmara enters the Strait of the Bosporus (17 miles long) do the winds pick up. Here, at the juncture of the Bosporus and Sea of Marmara, our merchant travelers see nothing more than a small fishing village. They do not know—have no way of discerning—that this will become one of the great cities of the world, Istanbul.

Passing up the Bosporus, our merchant adventurers finally come into the Black Sea. This is one of the great inland seas of the Eurasian continent, and they have come all this way to obtain metal and grain, products for which the region is justly famed. After spending several weeks on the Black Sea, they will return, passing by Troy once more. It is unlikely that they have it in for Troy, or that anyone is muttering that Troy (like latter-day Carthage) "must be destroyed," but the wealth and

ATLANTIS AND THE FLOOD

Many, if not most, early Middle Eastern societies have legends that speak of a universal flood, a catastrophe that marks a sharp divide between the before and after (hence the term *antediluvian*, meaning "before the flood"). A much smaller number of societies also speak of a lost continent, a highly developed civilization that was wiped out by a much smaller flood. Oddly enough, both legends may come from the same area: the eastern Mediterranean.

Scientists have long known that the island of Thera has an ancient volcano, one that blew off sometime in the Bronze Age. Thanks to more precise dating methods (including the study of the bristlecone tree, which lives for thousands of years), scientists now believe that the volcanic explosion at Thera can be dated to approximately 1627 B.C. If they are correct, then the wall of water coming from Thera wiped out the Minoan civilization a good 350 years before the Trojan War and "Idomeneus over there—standing with his Cretans" (as Helen expresses it in the *Iliad*) were descendants of a much earlier civilization. Thera is currently quiet, but there could be another volcanic explosion in its long-dormant cone.

Atlantis—as it is called—is a much trickier proposition, because, as many scientists explain, evidence of the disappearance of an entire continent would be everywhere. But what if Thera and the destruction of northern Crete were the foundation for the belief in the lost continent of Atlantis? Some scholars believe this is possible. The Great Flood is another matter.

prominence of the city have won it envy from around the Middle East. As they return to Crete, our merchant adventurers doubtless tell friends and relatives of the journey and its rewards. The most perilous part, they say, is being becalmed by the prevailing northeast wind in the vicinity of Troy.

Our landward visitors and our sea-based ones have completed a great circuit on our behalf. Through their eyes, we see that Troy—while not

In 1998, American geologists William Ryan and Walter Pitman published their work, *Noah's Flood: The New Scientific Discoveries About the Event That Changed History*. The two spent many years examining sedimentary deposits from various parts of the Mediterranean. One of their breakthrough moments was the realization that although the sea-level current pushes through the Strait of the Dardanelles and the Bosporus south, there is a deeper current, perhaps several hundred feet deep, that flows in just the opposite direction. Using conjecture as well as scientific analysis, Ryan and Pitman theorized that the near-universal tale of a Great Flood comes from a catastrophe that occurred approximately 7,600 years ago. Sometime in the fifth millennium B.C., the salt water of the Eastern Mediterranean broke through the land obstacles of what are now the Dardanelles, Sea of Marmara, and Bosporus. What we now call the Black Sea had been a huge freshwater lake, but in a matter of days it became an inland sea, connected to the Mediterranean. This, Ryan and Pitman postulate, would account for the dozens—if not hundreds—of tales of a great flood that displaced the men and women of the Late Stone Age.

Ryan and Pitman will almost certainly not have the last word on the matter. Scientific data continues to accumulate, and through dendachronology (the study of tree rings) and the study of the Greenland ice core, scientists will continue to develop new theories. The Ryan and Pitman theory is attractive, but it has not gained a consensus among climate scholars.

Troy's location on the Aegean Sea made the city powerful and rich. Passing merchants were forced to pay a toll to the city, and many of them disembarked to sell or trade their wares. Archaeologists digging in Troy discovered many artifacts that showed the considerable wealth of the city's inhabitants.

one of the great powers of the ancient Middle East—was nonetheless an important place, and that its royal family was one of the most fortunate to be found. Unlike the king of the Hittite Empire, for example, Troy did not need to maintain a standing army.

Or did it?

Arms
and Armor

There are times when the Late Bronze Age (2000–1200 B.C.) seems so far off that we cannot imagine men, women, and children acting in ways similar to us today. One of the great gifts of the *Iliad* and the *Odyssey* is their depiction of human beings who seem not too different from ourselves.

Let us begin with the men.

BRONZE AGE CHAMPIONS

Both from Homer and other sources, we have a good sense that the people of the Iron Age—which came after the Bronze—thought of their ancestors as greater men, almost superhuman. Perhaps it is because the Early Iron Age people realized that their technology was superior to that of their ancestors; how, then, they asked, could their great-great-great-grandfathers have achieved such amazing things?

How could they have:

- ◎ Built the massive beehive tombs (often called "treasuries") at Mycenae in Greece?
- ◎ Sailed across the wine-dark sea at a time when nautical knowledge was limited?
- ◎ Fought in great battles such as those on the plain of Troy?

The answer is that people can do much more than they believe. Often, when one poses these types of questions to people who have done something remarkable, their answer is that they did it because they did not know they were supposed to be incapable of the deed! Keeping this aspect of human behavior in mind, we look at the champions who fought in the so-called Trojan War (from the other side, it may well have been labeled the Greek War).

THE NINTH YEAR

Homer begins the *Iliad* with Book I, titled "The Rage of Achilles." Homer tells us that the war has already lasted nine long years and that the Greeks (or Achaeans) have been encamped on the beach for most of that time, only sending out war parties to pillage the towns of Troy's allies. Homer goes on to say that a quarrel between Agamemnon, the king of Mycenae, and Achilles, leader of the Myrmidons, has brought the Greek efforts to a standstill. As occasionally happens in the *Iliad*, a woman—or group of women—are to blame.

In one of the numerous raids conducted on nearby territories, the Greeks have despoiled, or violated, a sanctuary of the god Apollo. The god has therefore afflicted the Greeks, shooting arrows that bring sickness into their camp. To make good, and appease the god, the Greeks realize they must return one of the women they have taken from the god's sanctuary. Lord Agamemnon is called upon to return Chryseis, who has become his lover, and because he and Achilles are already at odds, Agamemnon demands that Achilles' slave woman, Bresieas, be delivered to his tent. This is the final straw, Achilles says. Although he allows Agamemnon's men to take the woman, Achilles vows that he and his Myrmidons—the best of Greek fighters—will sit out the contest.

This all sounds so silly, improbable. But is it possible?

The short answer is yes. Recent studies of Troy and Greece during the Late Bronze Age indicate that slave women were important booty, an inescapable part of the logic, or illogic, of war. In the Greek city of Pylos, for example, there were almost 1,500 slave women put to work harvesting flax, which was turned into linen. Because Pylos had one of the best-kept archives of Late Bronze Age times, we know that many of these were "women of Asia." We cannot say for certain that the encounter between Agamemnon and Achilles happened because of women, but we can declare it within the realm of possibility. The war, after all, is said to have commenced because of a single woman, the beautiful Helen.

BATTLE ON THE BEACH

Because Achilles sits out the battle, the Trojans do much better than usual. Led by their champion, Prince Hector (the elder brother of Paris), the Trojans push the Greeks back to their ships, and on one occasion come close to burning the vessels. It is here that Homer—ever the great narrator—brings in a relief party: the Myrmidons led by Patroclus.

Patroclus is a cousin of Achilles, and though not as skilled in war, he has been tutored by his kinsman. Knowing that Achilles is "sulking in his tent" (an expression made famous by Homer), and that the Trojans may bring complete disaster to the Greeks, Patroclus puts on Achilles' armor and leads the Myrmidons onto the field. As Homer describes it, Patroclus drives the Trojans back on all fronts, and three times he tries to scale Troy's walls, but each time he is pushed back by the god Apollo.

HELEN AS ARCHETYPE

For 2,800 years, listeners and readers have been entranced by the *Iliad* and the *Odyssey*, many of them asking, "Could the war have been launched by the abduction of one woman?" There is no definitive answer, because no set of bones has ever emerged with some type of "Helen" identification. We are much closer to the truth than ever before, however, and our progress is thanks both to archaeology and the imaginative pens of numerous writers.

In 1987, a series of wall paintings was found on the island of Thera, where a major volcano erupted about 1627 B.C. Wonderfully preserved, these frescoes give the modern viewer one of his or her first looks at the women of the Late Bronze Age. These are mostly upper-class women (not slaves), but they often perform tasks that we would today consider menial, such as harvesting saffron. The work belies their upper-class position, however, and the cosmetics on their faces indicates that these women had enough hours in the day to arrange and adorn themselves. Some of them would not be out of place on a modern fashion runway.

Hair color presents a surprise for the modern viewer. For almost a century, movie reviewers have decried the tendency to make

We moderns do not have to accept this view; instead, we can employ the archaeology of recent times to show that Troy's walls (some at least) sloped outward in such a way as to defy men like Patroclus. The climactic scene of the battle takes place when Hector—thinking that Patroclus is Achilles—takes a stand against the Greeks.

> Hector waiting, watching
> The greathearted Patroclus trying to stagger free,
> Seeing him wounded there with the sharp bronze
> Came rushing into him right across the lines
> And rammed his spearshaft home,
> Stabbing deep in the bowels, and the brazen point
> Went jutting straight out through Patroclus' back.

Helen, Cleopatra, and other Mediterranean-area women blondes or redheads. It was always believed that there were no blondes at the time. The frescoes show us the opposite, however. There definitely were blondes and redheads in the Aegean world, and these hair colors may have been much sought after, because they were out of the ordinary. We may never know if Helen was indeed a blonde or a redhead, but we can accept Homer's words about her appearance, knowing that they are indeed possible (he always describes Helen and her husband, Menelaus, as redhaired Spartans).

There is mischief in the faces on the frescoes, and the occasional hint of irony. These women know that they live in a man's world, but they are determined to make the best of it. How much silver or gold have some of their husbands offered to their families, for example? How long have these women held out before accepting marriage proposals? We may never know the answers to these questions, but mysteries like these are beginning to be unraveled.

Whether Helen is "real" or not, there were aristocratic women like her. The world of the *Iliad* and the *Odyssey* is becoming more visual for us today.

Now panic seized the Greeks. Seeing their champion—whom they believe to be Achilles—fall, they retreat to the ships. As often happens in the *Iliad*, Homer takes us away from the battle of the common man, and focuses on the words of a dying champion. Hector taunts Patroclus, saying:

> Surely you must have thought you'd storm my city down,
> You'd wrest from the wives of Troy their day of freedom,
> Drag them off in ships to your own dear fatherland—
> You fool!

Hector reminds Patroclus that the horse is sacred to Troy, and that his chariot team is better than any Greek one. He goes further, though, saying that he will leave Patroclus' body for the vultures to devour. Patroclus shouts back, however, letting Hector know that this moment of triumph will be short.

> Hector! Now is your time to glory to the skies . . .
> now the victory is yours,
> A gift of the son of Cronus, Zeus—Apollo too—
> they brought me down with all their deathless ease,
> *They* are the ones who tore the armor off my back.

To strip a foe of his armor was the ultimate insult, but it also may have been quite necessary in Bronze Age warfare. Bronze was time-consuming to produce, and the arms and armor of a fallen foe would make an important prize. Hector knew, however, that a great champion like Patroclus deserved to be buried *with* his arms and armor, much like an Egyptian pharaoh was buried with his servants, slaves, dogs, and cats. According to Homer, Hector gets the armor, and he exults over the body of Patroclus, but he is not swift enough to catch the magnificent racing stallions that belong to Achilles. They escape, with their chariot, and "swift Achilles" (as Homer often calls him) will surely return for vengeance.

SAVING THE DAY

Achilles has sulked in his tent so long that he does not rise to the occasion immediately. There is grave danger to the Greek ships—as the Trojans surge forward—and this time it is Menelaus, king of Sparta, who rallies the Greeks. He does not have the magic armor of Achilles, or the favor

The hero Achilles was a teacher and friend to his kinsman, Patroclus, who tried to rally the Greeks in his cousin's absence. During the battle, Hector kills Patroclus and earns the wrath of Achilles. This clay pot depicts Achilles tending to Patroclus's wounds.

of any god or goddess; Menelaus is simply a man who has lost his wife to another and who wants her back.

Thanks to Menelaus, the Greeks rally to defend the ships. One can question whether the Trojans really should have tried to burn them; lacking a means of returning home, the Greeks would have become more desperate, not less. The most important thing is that the Greeks live to fight another day, and a shaky truce is established between Achilles and Agamemnon. The former will return to the battlefield.

THE GREATEST DUEL

Throughout the *Iliad*, one feels the impending doom of Hector. A fantastic fighter he is, but it is Achilles who is favored by the gods. In the last, dying moments of Patroclus, Homer has the Greek warning Hector of his imminent destruction.

Furious over his cousin's death and the way that Hector stripped the armor from the corpse, Achilles presents himself at the head of the Greek army. As is often the case, the rank and file of both armies disappear from view, and the narrator takes his listener directly to the two champions: Hector and Achilles. The former is a man's man, made for war, but the latter simply *lives* for conflict. One can imagine Hector sitting by the fireside one day, content to let younger men perform the heroics; not so Achilles.

Homer takes his listener—and the modern reader—to the palace of Priam, where Andromache, the wife of Hector, begs her husband not to venture out of the city walls. Holding his one-year-old baby in her arms, Andromache (who has come to represent the aristocratic women of Troy) asks her husband what good will come if he is slain? Is it not better to forego the heroics, she asks, and to stay safely within the walls? Even Achilles cannot batter them down. Eventually, the Greeks will come to their senses, realize that the siege is hopeless, and depart.

Hector knows better. The meeting with Achilles has been preordained by the gods. He, a mere mortal, cannot put it off. Perhaps Hector holds out a slim chance (very slim indeed) that he can prevail, but for the most part he seems resigned to his fate. Taking off his magnificent helmet, Hector holds his son in his arms, understanding that this is very likely the last time he shall see his family.

Hector steps outside the Scaean Gates. He is alone.

GORY TRIUMPH

Achilles comes roaring up in his chariot, and even Hector, who has always shown bravery, feels his courage fail him. Turning, Hector runs literally around the walls of Troy three times (archaeologists would later retrace his steps), trying to get away from the man-killing machine, Achilles. But finally, knowing there is no escape, Hector returns to the main gates to await his foe. As Achilles approaches, Hector makes one last plea:

> Come, we'll swear to the gods, the highest witnesses—
> The gods will oversee our binding pacts. I swear
> I will never mutilate you—merciless as you are—
> If Zeus allows me to last it out and tear your life away.
> But once I've stripped your glorious armor, Achilles,
> I will give your body back to your loyal comrades.
> Swear you'll do the same.

The reader—or listener—knows what will come next.

> Hector, stop!
> You unforgivable, you . . . don't talk to me of pacts.
> There are no binding oaths between men and lions—
> Wolves and lambs can enjoy no meeting of the minds—
> They are all bent on hating each other to the death.
> So with you and me.

And the fight begins.

Hector is known for his skill, but he is no match for godlike Achilles. The fight lasts longer than it would with any other man, but Hector is eventually stabbed through the chest. He calls out, again, for his enemy to show mercy, to deliver his body to his father, but Achilles shakes his head in fury. When Hector is dead, Achilles pierces his ankle tendons and runs ropes through them. Securing the other end of the ropes to his chariot, Achilles races round the walls of Troy, showing the ruined body of Hector to the horrified populace.

In all of Homer—the *Iliad* and the *Odyssey*—there is no comparable moment.

A PACT

The Trojans are appalled by the fall of their great hero, but King Priam and Princess Anromache suffer the most. Both had sensed the inevitability of Hector's death, but it still came as a terrible wrench. Worst of all was that Achilles kept possession of Hector's body, denying his slain foe the right to a proper burial.

As Homer explains it, King Priam undertakes one of the most desperate, and heroic, of all actions in the Trojan War. Under cover of night, he leaves his lofty citadel, steals through one of Troy's gates, and makes

Disguised as a commoner, King Priam sneaks into the tent of the hero Achilles, where he kisses the hands that have killed his beloved son, Hector. The meeting between the old man and the young hero is one of the most poignant sections of the *Iliad*.

his way—stealthily—to the tent of man-slaying Achilles. When the Greek champion awakes, he finds an elderly man kissing his hands. When Achilles demands to know why, the old man says that he has just performed an unspeakable act: He has kissed the hands that deprived his son of life.

Raising old Priam up to his own level, Achilles sits with the king for several hours. Priam explains his need: He must give his son a proper burial, or else Hector will be denied entrance to the afterlife. Reminding Achilles that he, too, has a father, one who would mourn, Priam asks, time and again, for the body of Hector. In the end, Achilles agrees. Not only will he return Hector's corpse, but there will be a seven-day truce between Greeks and Trojans, so that the former may pay full attention to Patroclus' funeral, and the Trojans can do the same with Hector. There are no pacts between men and lions, Achilles had said, but there was one between a rather young man and a very old one, both of whom had seen enough of the tragedy of war.

The *Iliad* ends with an immortal line:

"And so the Trojans buried Hector breaker of horses."

Homeward Bound

God scattered the Akhaians.
— King Nestor to Telemachus, the *Odyssey*

Travelers the world over know the axiom that the return journey is more difficult than the original one. Generally speaking, the traveler is weary, anxious to reach home, and the miles (whether land-based or nautical) seem to drag as he or she retraces his or her steps. This was certainly the case with the Greeks returning from Troy.

THE OFFENSE

Homer tells us, in different parts of the *Odyssey*, that the Greeks violated certain fundamental laws in the days and hours that followed the sack of Troy. Some of the Greeks committed unspeakable acts against Trojan civilians, while other Greeks—including some of the great heroes—acted as if it was they (not the gods and goddesses) who had accomplished the great deed. Even Odysseus—considered the cleverest of all the Greeks—offended a god, Poseidon. As with the siege and sack of Troy, Homer is our greatest guide, but historians and archaeologists have done their best, over time, to use the meager physical evidence to contradict him on some points, and to embrace his telling on certain other ones.

The *Odyssey*, which, like the *Iliad*, was originally sung and only later put onto clay tablets, begins with the lamentations of the goddess Athena. Watching the terrible trials that the hero Odysseus has endured (he is currently a love prisoner of the goddess Circe), Athena asks her father, Zeus—the greatest of all the gods—if she can help Odysseus return home. Zeus is not at all averse; he remembers that Odysseus is the most clever and adroit of heroes. The way in which Homer lays out the scene indicates, however, that he—and most of the Greeks of his time—believed that men and women had to work out their own salvation. The gods and goddesses could assist humans, but the brunt of the work had to come from human hands.

Descending from Mount Olympus, home of the gods, to the island kingdom of Ithaca, the goddess Athena puts on a male human countenance. She goes to the palace of Odysseus and meets his 20-year-old son, Telemachus, who had been born just before his father had to leave for the Trojan War. Athena sees that the palace and home of Odysseus—as well as his island kingdom—are in danger from a host of suitors, men who have come to vie for the hand of Queen Penelope. She has kept them at bay for years with a variety of clever stratagems, but their patience has worn thin. Eventually, she will have to choose one of them, and in the meantime, the suitors are slowly devouring the meat, drink, and substance of Odysseus' home.

Disguised, Athena presents herself to Telemachus as one who has known Odysseus during the siege of Troy. His father is not dead, she assures Telemachus. It is time, she says, for the 20-year-old son to leave home, to quest in search of his father. Knowing that the departure will cause his mother grief, as well as put the offensive suitors on their guard, Telemachus steals away from the island of Ithaca, headed south by southeast. Athena has urged him to seek out "that noble sage of Pylos," King Nestor, and then to seek "Menelaus, the red-haired king of Sparta." These are the oldest and wisest of the Greeks who have returned from Troy. If anyone can help Telemachus in his quest, it is them.

Half realizing that he has spoken with a goddess in disguise, Telemachus sets out with 20 oarsmen (one for each year of his age).

THE OLD CHAMPIONS

Telemachus reaches "sandy Pylos," the home of King Nestor on the western side of Greece. There, he meets and is greeted by old King Nestor, one of the few Greeks that made it home without any major calamities. The aged king soon recognizes Telemachus; the son's features and noble

One of King Menelaus's strongest allies was Odysseus, a king who conceived the plan that ultimately defeated the Trojans. Having offended Poseidon, the god of the sea, Odysseus was condemned to wander the earth for 10 years while men vied for his kingdom and his wife Penelope (*above*).

mind clearly resemble those of Odysseus. When Telemachus asks for specific news of his father, Nestor replies with what he knows—nearly all of it sorrowful.

> When we plundered Priam's town and tower
> And took to the ships, God scattered the Akhaians.
> He had a mind to make homecoming hard for them,
> Seeing they would not think straight or behave,
> Or some would not. So evil days came upon them.

Nestor had been there on the beach, along with Agamemnon, Odysseus, and the son of Achilles. The Greeks had not made the proper sacrifices to the gods, believing that it was the might of their arms alone that had conquered Troy. The gods and goddesses had been upset, and their displeasure soon turned to a cold fury.

At dawn we dragged our ships to the lordly water,
Stowed away all our plunder
And the slave women in their low hip girdles.
But half the army elected to stay behind
With Agamemnon as their corps commander;
The other half embarked and pulled away.
We made good time, the huge sea smoothed before us.

This was but the beginning, however. As Homer expresses it—through the words of King Nestor—the voyage home was one despair-filled moment after another. Sometimes the sea rose with great, crashing force, and at other times the winds behaved in contrary ways. Nestor made it safe to Pylos, for which he thanked his lucky stars, but Menelaus, the king of Sparta, was blown hundred of miles off course. Departing from what Homer calls the "wine-dark sea" (the Aegean), Menelaus was blown into the Great South Sea (the waters between Crete and Egypt). There he had spent many years and had only recently returned.

Menelaus was still alive, at least. The same could not be said for his brother Agamemnon, lord of Mycenae. Agamemnon had offended the gods by taking a daughter of King Priam, Princess Cassandra, home from Troy. As a servant of the god Apollo, Cassandra had special protection, something that Agamemnon chose to ignore. Just hours after his return, the lordly Agamemnon was stabbed by his unfaithful wife and her lover. His wife, naturally, claimed there was justification sufficient for such a deed. Agamemnon had sacrificed their daughter, Iphigenia, at the very beginning of the Trojan War.

Parts of the terrible story were already known to Telemachus, but the words of Nestor made him certain of the gloomy, sometimes terrible fates that befell so many heroes of the Trojan War. Still knowing nothing of his father's situation, Telemachus decided to continue on his journey to Sparta to meet "red-haired" Menelaus, the king whose wife was Helen (she whose abduction had caused the war in the first place). King Nestor agreed, handing Telemachus a fine chariot and one of his sons to accompany him on the landward journey to Sparta. As Homer expresses it, several days of furious chariot driving resulted in the two men coming to the "grainlands of Lakedaimon."

Menelaus and Helen gave Telemachus a royal welcome. Like Nestor, they were swift to recognize the features of Odysseus in his 20-year-old son. Menelaus and Helen appeared to be completely reconciled; there seemed no holdover of bitterness between them for all the actions that had transpired since her abduction. Menelaus had little to say about Odysseus other than words of great praise; the best he could do was acquaint Telemachus with all the terrible trials he, Helen, and their Spartan group had experienced since the sack of Troy, 10 long years ago.

> During my first try at a passage homeward
> The gods detained me, tied me down to Egypt—
> For I had been too scant in hekatombs,
> And gods will have the rules each time remembered.
> There is an island washed by the open sea
> Lying off Nile mouth—seamen call it Pharos—
> Distant a day's sail in a clean hull.

MEDITERRANEAN GEOGRAPHY IN THE *ODYSSEY*

Homer was a poet, first and foremost, intent on keeping the attention of his audience. So well did he achieve his goal that he has been read for the past 2,800 years. Scholars who pore over the *Odyssey* naturally look for clues, ways to determine if Homer was also an accurate reporter of his time. Though he certainly misses the mark on some occasions, there are some startling correlations between what Homer sang about 2,800 years ago and what we know of the Mediterranean today. Consider these expressions:

"The wine-dark sea" (Homer's description of the Aegean)

"The fish-cold sea" (his description of the waters between Crete and Egypt)

"The Great South Sea" (very likely his description of the waters between Italy and Africa)

"The sunburned land" (very likely Homer's description of what are now Israel and Lebanon)

Whether Homer heard the descriptions from men who had come before him, or whether he had traveled in his youth is difficult

There, Menelaus and his Spartans were marooned for some time (Homer is not explicit about the precise length). When he learned that the gods were offended by his lack of piety, Menelaus went deep into Egypt, perhaps to Thebes, to perform ritual sacrifices so he might return home. Even then, his wish was not immediately granted. Years passed, and Menelaus and his Spartans grew rich through the Egyptian trade, but always they longed for home, for passage over the "fish-cold sea." Finally the gods relented, and Menelaus and Helen returned to Sparta. Pleased as they were to finally reach their goal, the king and queen were dismayed to learn that Agamemnon had been killed. Even the revenge carried out by Agamemnon's son, Orestes, did not remove the bitterness felt by Menelaus over his brother's demise.

to say. Some of his descriptions are so apt, so poignant, however, that it is impossible to improve upon them. Not only does Homer provide us with insight into Mediterranean lands and waters, he also describes, in passing, material items that give us clues as to the lives of the Greeks, and perhaps the Trojans as well. Consider these:

"rawhide sandals"

"two-handled jugs and barley meal"

"discus throw and javelin"

"chariot horses and a polished car"

All these expressions come from the *Odyssey*, and, even though Homer lived 400 years after the events of the Trojan War, he seems an accurate reporter of the material life of the time. We moderns are not that surprised to hear that the discus and javelin were used so early in Greek competitions, but the "two-handled jugs" describe the Mycenaean pottery so well that one wonders if Homer really just threw it in for color, or if he intended his future listeners to gauge his veracity.

Telemachus spent several days at the Spartan court. The listener of Homer's day and the reader of ours gets to hear Helen speak, and there are some intriguing parallels between what she told King Priam and what she says to Menelaus and Telemachus, 10 years later:

> The Trojan women raised a cry—but my heart
> Sang—for I had come round, long before,
> To dreams of sailing home, and I repented
> The mad day [the goddess] Aphrodite
> Drew me away from my dear fatherland,
> Forsaking all—child, bridal bed, and husband.

Homer is brilliantly ambiguous concerning Helen. Was she indeed a helpless victim, dragged to Troy and thereby the innocent cause of the terrible war? Had she been content during her 10 years in Troy? Were she and Menelaus truly as well reconciled as Homer suggests? Like any great narrator, Homer leaves his listeners with some doubts, things they must decide for themselves.

FATHER AND SON RETURN

As Homer explains it, the goddess Athena has done her best to assure the return of Odysseus. He has been captivated by a minor goddess for years, but he wins his freedom and sails for Ithaca (with plenty more adventures along the way). Meanwhile, Athena comes back to earth in human guise to urge Telemachus, also, to also return to Ithaca, for the most important hour of his family's life is at hand.

Cast up on the shore of the island which he had once called home, Odysseys is extremely careful. He meets and is befriended by a goatherd, one who knew and loved him in the past but does not recognize him. By all wonders, Telemachus returns just days later, and he, too, arrives at the goatherdsman's hut, where father and son are reunited.

Odysseus has taken pains, to this point, to avoid being recognized by anyone. In the first minutes of meeting his son, Odysseus manages to carry on a charade of types, speaking as if he knew Odysseus. Finally, overcome with emotion, Odysseus reveals his true identity to Telemachus.

> I am that father whom your boyhood lacked
> And suffered pain for lack of. I am he.

These touching lines are equaled at only one other point. Days later, when Odysseus, in disguise, crosses the threshold of his former home, his faithful dog, Argos, recognizes his master's voice, even though 20 years have passed.

An old hound, lying near, pricked up his ears
And lifted up his muzzle. This was Argos,
Trained as a puppy by Odysseus,
But never taken on a hunt before
His master sailed for Troy.

Odysseus is nearly overcome by the sentiment shown by his pet, but he has little time to rejoice. The old dog dies—very likely from a stroke—in the very moment that Odysseus crosses into his home.

THE RECKONING

The final part of the *Odyssey* is a grim tale. Knowing that the suitors would gladly kill them, Odysseus and Telemachus have to use cunning and guile. Odysseus takes his time revealing his true identity to Penelope, and, as with his son, he does not do so immediately. Meanwhile, father and son have laid a terrible trap for the suitors.

Penelope announces that she is finally ready to choose from among the suitors. She will marry the man who can string Odysseus' famous bow, she says. One after another, the suitors come forth, but they all fail in the attempt. Finally, an ill-dressed traveler (Odysseus in disguise) asks to have a try. Stringing the bow, he reveals his identity, and—with the help of his son and faithful servants—he kills all of the suitors.

Even after father and son have dispatched dozens of men, sending them to terrible deaths, Odysseus' bloodlust is not satisfied, and it requires an intervention by the goddess Athena to bring him to his senses. The moral is clear. Insults and degradation (such as those perpetrated by the suitors) must be avenged, but it is all too easy for one to go too far in vengeance.

Finally reunited with Penelope, who has held out through 20 long years (10 for the siege of Troy and 10 for her husband's long return), Odysseus also goes to meet his aged father. The reunion of father and son is the final set piece of the *Odyssey*, the book that picks up where the *Iliad* left off. Homer has done something quite remarkable, making the lives of men and women of the Bronze Age real and vivid for us today. It is our

The *Odyssey* concludes with Odysseus returning to Ithaca to reclaim his family and his throne. In a contest to win Penelope's hand, Odysseus strings a bow that once belonged to him and then promptly slays the men who tried to take his place in his absence.

misfortune that he does not address what happened to the Trojans after the sack of their city.

THE MODERN INTERPRETATION

Anyone who spends much time with the *Iliad* and the *Odyssey* comes away with a deeper appreciation of what it means to be human. This is part of the magic of Homer. Our modern-day reading naturally begs the question, however: Was the *Odyssey* in any sense real? Did the heroes of the Trojan War truly experience such wanderings, heartbreaks, and episodes of violence?

We believe that this is the case.

No historian today would boldly say that Odysseus was real or that Agamemnon died at the hand of his wife and her lover, only to be avenged by his son. Historians, archaeologists, and philologists (those who study ancient texts) have to be more careful in their assessments. What they *would* venture is that the *Odyssey* speaks to, and is in an analogous way a history of, the end of the Late Bronze Age, a time when men and women of all types and nations were cast adrift in a terrible time of upheaval.

Consider the following facts, established by well more than a century of archaeological work:

- ☼ The Hittite Empire practically ceased to exist by about 1150 B.C.
- ☼ The Egyptian kingdom was threatened by numerous invaders at the same time.
- ☼ The Mycenaean Empire came to a sudden, abrupt end.
- ☼ The palaces at Mycenae, Tiryns, Pylos, as well as Troy were all burned sometime between about 1250 and 1150 B.C.

So great, so immense were these changes that the historian Robert Drews, in *The End of the Bronze Age*, calls them simply "The Catastrophe." In his words: "The end of the eastern Mediterranean Bronze Age, in the twelfth century B.C. was one of history's most frightful turning points. For those who experienced it, it was a calamity."

Civilization did not disappear after 1150 B.C., but it went through a long metamorphosis. When Homer sang of heroes and of cities, of the Trojan War and its aftermath, he was on the other side of a great divide. Homer lived in the early part of the Age of Iron. Looking back across four centuries, he saw many notable and noble things about the past, but one suspects he was pleased not to have to fight in Late Bronze Age wars.

Troy Forgotten

No other bard or historian of the Trojan War is known. To us moderns, looking back across 3,200 years, it seems as if Troy and its war were simply forgotten for about 400 years, only to be resurrected by Homer.

THE GREEKS RETURN

Mycenaean civilization collapsed shortly after the Trojan War. The glorious era of palaces like those at Mycenae, Argos, and Pylos was over. That did not mean that the Greeks disappeared, however.

Today it remains controversial whether the Greeks of Homer's time were direct descendants of the Mycenaeans, or if Greece had been substantially repopulated by other migrant groups, including the Dorians. In either case, the Greeks of Homer's time showed a strong interest in Anatolia, or Asia Minor, and Greek settlements began cropping up on the west side of what is now Turkey.

The Greeks had always been fishermen. In the ninth and eighth centuries B.C., they expanded their nets to become colonists on the coast of Asia Minor. The city of Halicarnassus, which may have been the birthplace of Homer, was settled by about 850 B.C., and numerous other inlets and isles of the Turkish coast were soon populated by Greeks. Looking at the map today, it is easy to see why. The coast of Asia Minor had many raw materials, which the Greeks desired. More, by having towns on both sides of the "wine-dark sea," the Greeks established the beginnings of a commercial empire.

As the Trojans had learned centuries earlier, having an empire could be perilous.

THE PERSIAN WARS

The Hittite Empire collapsed about 1150 B.C. There was no replacement for the Hittites in Asia Minor. Not until 530 B.C. did another major power come to dominate what is now Turkey. This power was the Persians, whose empire was founded by Cyrus and continued by Darius and Xerxes.

The Persians came from what is now Iran, and the affairs of Asia Minor and Greece were not that important to the well-being of their empire. When the Persians extended their rule to Asia Minor, however, the Greek city-states along the west coast rose in rebellion, acting as the proximate cause for the Greek-Persian Wars. The conflicts began in 494 B.C., when Miletus rose against its Persian overlords. One of the most notable dates in Western military history came four years later, when the Athenians defeated the Persians on a narrow beach called Marathon, 26 miles from their city. To the Greek way of thinking, Marathon should have been the beginning and the end, but to the Persians, long accustomed to triumph, it was but the beginning. Ten years later, in the spring of 480 B.C., Xerxes, the king of kings, arrived at the Dardanelles with an immense army of Persians and their allies. Various historians have estimated the Persian army at as many as 1.6 million men, but it is extremely unlikely that such a number could have been fed, much less clothed, commanded, and driven on to Greece. Even the more conservative estimate of 300,000 seems very large.

For our purpose, the Greek-Persian Wars (and the great battles at Thermopylae, Salamis, and Plataea) are less important than the attention paid to Troy. According to the Greek historian Herodotus (who lived about 50 years later), Xerxes had a special passion concerning Troy. He insisted on seeing the place and sacrificing 1,000 black bulls on the spot. Xerxes saw himself as the champion of Asia and Asia Minor, come to chastise the Greeks who had once sacked Troy. Xerxes had a bridge of boats built across the Dardanelles, and his vast army departed from Troy, on its way to sack and burn Athens.

The king of kings did not prevail, however. His fleet was nearly destroyed at the Battle of Salamis, and Xerxes had to beat a hasty, undignified retreat. Arriving at the western side of the Dardanelles, he found that the bridge of boats had been destroyed by a storm. The king of kings and his men were ferried back to safety in Asia Minor.

One hundred and fifty years passed.

After the Trojan War, many years and several civilizations passed before anyone thought of using Troy again. The great Persian king Xerxes (*above, with Queen Esther*) was enamored with the forgotten city and launched a military campaign against Greece from the Trojan shore.

ALEXANDER THE GREAT

In 336 B.C., Alexander, the king of Macedon, began an invasion of the Persian Empire. Born and raised Macedonian (not Greek), Alexander nevertheless identified with Greek civilization. He saw Xerxes' invasion of Greece 150 years earlier as a crime, and he was inspired by Homer. It is said that Alexander slept with a copy of the *Iliad* under his pillow.

There was no bridge of boats for Alexander and the Macedonians. They crossed by boat, and Alexander made a point of standing in the foremost one and throwing his spear to the land before getting into the shallow water. This was his way of announcing that he had come to conquer Asia. It was also a symbol that he saw himself as the new Achilles.

Like Xerxes before him, Alexander was fascinated by Troy. The Greek historian Arrian tells us that Alexander visited the Tomb of Achilles (a huge mound that everyone assumed was a warrior's burial place) and that he paced the steps of windy Troy, time and again, so as to claim he had stood where Achilles and Hector had fought, and where Helen and King Priam had observed the Greek champions. Like Xerxes, Alexander offered prayers and sacrifices. To everyone there, it was apparent that he wanted to conquer in the other direction. Xerxes had failed to avenge the Trojan loss of their city. Alexander meant to complete what his Bronze Age heroes had begun.

During the next four years, Alexander dismantled the Persian Empire. He defeated King Darius III at Issus, and then at Guagamela. He captured the Phoenician city of Tyre, even though it was half a mile off the mainland. By 332 B.C., Alexander had entered Babylon as its conqueror. Though earlier Middle Eastern monarchs, such as Sargon I, Hammurabai, and Shalmaneser, had claimed to be lords of the known world, Alexander had by far the best claim.

What about Troy, however?

The town on the south side of the Dardanelles did not rise to its former prominence. Thanks to Alexander's empire (which did not long survive its master), Troy was briefly at the crossroads, a place for messengers from Babylon to Greece and back again. Aside from Alexander's visit, Troy itself was of little importance, though. That was how it remained for the next 250 years, a time when the locals called it Ilion (Greek), rather than Troy. The footsteps of yet another conqueror were required to bring life back to Troy.

JULIUS AND AUGUSTUS CAESAR

Julius Caesar (100–44 B.C.) was a great Roman conqueror who defeated practically every foe he ever encountered. Not only was Caesar inspired by the Trojan War; he said that his family line descended from the Trojans who had escaped the destruction of their city. If Caesar had a personal hero, it was Alexander the Great. Like Alexander, Caesar found it important to visit Troy. On his campaign against the Pontic king, Mithradates, in 51 B.C., Caesar went to Troy, where, like Alexander, he paced the ground and measured the ramparts (his calculations have not survived). As a patriotic Roman, Caesar may not have wished to venerate the stories of Greek champions, but even so, his visit gave new life to the town, which was then called Ilium (Latin form of Ilion). Caesar paid little more attention to Troy, but after his assassination in 44 B.C., there was a renewed interest in the Trojan War.

VIRGIL

The Roman poet Virgil (who was a contemporary of both Julius and Augustus Caesar) saw his own time as rather plain and boring, or perhaps lacking in virtue when compared to earlier ones. Virgil took as his subject the Trojans that had escaped from their city as it burned, and he created a national epic for the Romans to rival that of Homer.

Virgil's great epic, the *Aeneid*, begins with these lines:

Wars and a man I sing—an exile driven on by Fate,
he was the first to flee the coast of Troy,
destined to reach Lavinian shores and Italian soil,
yet many blows he took on land and sea from the gods above.

Virgil lived about 700 years after Homer, and whatever information he had about the siege of Troy, and the city's fall, came from the earlier poet. Virgil did not intend to compete with Homer, however. He wanted

VIRGIL'S TROJANS

One has to remember that Virgil lived about 1,200 years after the events of the Trojan War. Otherwise, one might think that he was an eyewitness to the siege and fall of Priam's city.

Virgil does much more than Homer with the story of the Trojan Horse. Virgil describes how the horse is left on the great plain of Troy and how the Trojans debate over whether to bring it into the city. There are plenty who are against this idea, but their objections are overcome when a Trojan priest, Laocoon, is devoured by two sea serpents (he had been among those that resisted the idea). According to Virgil:

Smooth running rollers
We wheel beneath its hoofs, and heavy hempen ropes
We bind around its neck, and teeming with men-at-arms
The huge deadly engine climbs our city walls . . .
And round it boys and unwed girls sing hymns,
thrilled to lay a hand on the dangling ropes

to make an epic worthy of Rome and to demonstrate that Rome was the heir of ancient Troy.

Whether the reader is a first-century Roman or a modern-day American, one is struck by the skillful means by which Virgil depicts the destruction of Troy. Through his words, the reader sees Priam's towers collapse and most of the royal family put to the sword. Aeneas is one of the few that can escape, and realizing this, he gathers his family. His elderly father does not wish to leave, saying that he will die with the ruined city, but a sign from the gods—perhaps a thunderclap—persuades him otherwise. Placing an ox hide on his shoulders, Aeneas has his aged father get on his back, and, with his wife and young son in tow, the Trojan hero makes for safety. Somewhere outside the city, he suddenly realizes that his wife has been left behind. Turning back, Aeneas is ready to meet his doom, but a shade (or ghostly shadow) of his wife persuades him to continue the flight. According to Virgil, Aeneas and his family gather

---

As on and on it comes, gliding into the city,
looming high over the city's heart.

That night, the Greeks descend from their hiding place in the wooden horse to open the gates to their countrymen, who have sailed back under cover of darkness. The slaughter that follows is terrific, as portrayed by Virgil.

But all in the house is turmoil, misery, groans,
The echoing chambers ring with cries of women,
Wails of mourning hit the golden stars.
Mothers scatter in panic down the palace halls
And embrace the pillars, cling to them, kiss them hard.

No one has ever described the sack of Troy—or any other ancient world city—better than this. Virgil gives a very human face to the disaster that befell Priam's city.

the other Trojan refugees, and they begin what is a grand epic—akin to that of Odysseus. Many years are spent in traversing the Mediterranean, before Aeneas and the Trojans land in Italy. There, they become the ancestors of the Romans.

AUGUSTUS

Augustus, the first Roman emperor, knew Virgil. The poet sometimes went to the imperial palace to recite in front of the emperor and his family. When Virgil died at the age of fifty-one, the emperor made certain that the famous epic would be remembered. Augustus felt a strong affiliation with Troy, at least its ruins. He had been there while on a military campaign in 32 B.C.

During the long reign of Augustus (27 B.C. through A.D. 14) the Romans came to identify themselves as the descendants of Aeneas and their city as the new Troy. *This* Troy would not fall to the Greeks, or anyone else, they declared.

Troy itself fell into disrepair, however, and the sites were seldom visited after the first century A.D.

THE LATE ROMAN EMPIRE

Troy never made a major appearance again, at least not in Roman times. Virgil's epic was enough to keep the name in the minds of all educated Romans, but the place itself was of little interest. There was one great missed opportunity, when, in about 315, Emperor Constantine went looking to build a second Rome (the first had fallen on hard times). Constantine briefly considered the site of new Ilium, closer to the shore than old Troy, but he eventually settled on the little fishing village called Byzantium. It was renamed in his honor and remained Constantinople for the next thousand years. The last significant mention of Troy in Roman records shows that a Catholic bishop had his seat there about the year 520.

The Western world was in the throes of a major crisis.

THE DARK AGES

This name has its problems, because the modern reader assumes that it means there was little light, or knowledge, between about 550 and 750. In fact, the term *Dark Ages* means that we, the moderns can see very little as we look back. There is a lack of sources—both written and other—from

Alexander the Great, a fan of the *Iliad*, was determined to expand his empire beyond Greece and set his sights on Asia. After a short visit to Troy and Achilles' tomb, he went on to defeat Darius III (*above*), the royal descendant of Xerxes.

the Dark Ages, but it does not mean that the people of that time considered themselves as living in darkness!

Troy did disappear, in that people forgot where it had once stood. Anyone who recited Homer or Virgil knew that it was near the mouth of the Dardanelles, but that was about as close as they came. Surprisingly enough, the Dark Ages were not unkind to the story of Troy, however; dozens, if not hundreds of tribal chieftains in Germany, France, and other parts of northern Europe began to claim that they—like the Romans—were descended from Aeneas and those who had escaped from Troy. So frequently was this asserted that it seems it was a rare Dark Ages leader who did not claim some connection with ancient Troy. The real renaissance of Troy would begin in the High Middle Ages, though, a time when writing came back into fashion and when the ancient sources

(Homer, Hesiod, Herodotus, Virgil, and others) were brought back into the light.

ENGLAND, FRANCE, AND GERMANY

All three nations, and peoples, showed interest in Troy during the High Middle Ages. The Holy Roman Emperors often claimed direct descent from Aeneas. The kings of England and France claimed, as best they could, some sort of more convoluted descent. Oddly enough, almost none of the European leaders claimed to be descended from the *Greek* heroes. It is not too much to say that ancient Greece was out of fashion in the High Middle Ages and that ancient Rome was very much in favor.

One more great conquest was about to take place.

THE OTTOMAN EMPIRE

In 1353, the Ottoman Turks—an Asiatic people who had migrated westward over the preceding 200 years—conquered the area around Troy. They did not pay any special attention to the ruins, which may have been deeply buried, but the Ottomans claimed that they were the newest chapter in the long series of wars between Asia Minor and Europe. When they conquered Constantinople in 1453, the Ottomans renamed it Istanbul. They also declared that the Trojans had been avenged, that East had again conquered West.

Heinrich Schliemann

I had to extract, conceal and send away in such haste in order to withdraw them from the greed of my workers *(emphasis added).*
 —Heinrich Schliemann describing his discovery of
 Trojan gold

Historians, philologists, and musicians have dubbed the early nineteenth century the "Romantic Era" because its leading exemplars—persons like Beethoven, Schiller, and Goethe—eschewed the severe rationalism of an earlier time. One thing that the Romantic Era spawned was an increased interest in the past, its romantic elements most especially.

GREECE AND TURKEY

Both ancient Greece and ancient Asia Minor were on the minds of the European Romantics. The Ottoman Turks had conquered Greece back in the fifteenth century, and many European liberals (liberal and romantic often went hand in hand) ached to see a rebirth of Greek freedom. The long and bitter Greek Revolution was fought in the second and third decades of the nineteenth century, and only when England and France intervened at the naval Battle of Navarino did it become apparent that Greece would win its freedom from the Ottoman Turkish Empire. Once Greece accomplished this, European Romantics became more interested than ever in tales of Troy and the Trojan War; they saw that conflict as the beginning of three millennia of conflict between East and West.

Heinrich Schliemann was born in 1822, while the Greek Revolution was in full swing. Later in life, he attributed an illustration from a book as the source of his lifelong interest in the Trojans and Troy.

YOUNG SCHLIEMANN

Heinrich Schliemann grew up in northern Germany, the son of an impoverished Protestant pastor. Schliemann's father was undoubtedly a man of intelligence and skill, but he felt frustrated by his position in life, and he hoped for much greater things for his son. When Schliemann was about nine years old, his father read to him from an edition of Virgil's *Aeneid,* and father and son were transfixed by the illustration of Aeneas escaping from ruined Troy. Many years later, Schliemann claimed that he and his father had mutually agreed that day that the former would one day excavate Troy. Although numerous scholars have pointed out discrepancies in Schliemann's descriptions of that moment, it is not an unlikely one. Many children have fastened onto the idea or notion that will govern the rest of their lives at an early moment in childhood development.

The young Schliemann may have wished to go search for Troy at once, but he faced a dilemma that would become even more severe for those who eventually followed in his footsteps: the lack of money. Archaeology was not a science, or even an academic discipline. There were no schools or college departments of archaeology, and the handful of persons who were making their names in the field were usually rich men's sons. Schliemann did not possess this advantage, but he was determined not to let this hinder him. Therefore, he set out to become rich.

MAN OF BUSINESS

Schliemann was a pastor's son, but he showed a strong appetite for a business career. Starting out as a grocer, he moved to Amsterdam to become a clerk in a prominent Dutch import-export firm. Moving up rapidly, Schliemann became the firm's agent in Moscow and St. Petersburg, where he showed a keen eye for detail and a powerful passion for wealth. Prospering in the indigo trade, he was independently wealthy by the time the American gold rush began in 1848.

Like thousands of other Germans, Schliemann went to California. Unlike most of the others, he actually made a fortune. Schliemann did not pan for gold in the mountains and rivers of California; he bought and sold mining equipment, for which there was a steady, increasing market. Later, he weighed and assayed gold dust, and by the time he returned to the East Coast of the United States, he was very wealthy.

The battle for Greek independence from the Ottoman Empire inspired a revival of interest in ancient Greek culture and art. Heinrich Schliemann, a German born in 1822, was exposed to Virgil's *Aeneid* at an early age and was determined to become an archaeologist so he could excavate the treasures of Troy.

When he returned to Europe in 1851, he was a very rich man. That was not all, however.

Schliemann returned to Europe just as the Crimean War began, pitting Russia against the Ottoman Turks, England, and France. Schliemann ran food supplies for the British and French armies throughout the war; if he was rich at its beginning, he emerged from that contest with a great fortune. He would never have to work again.

Schliemann could have sat back, and rested on his laurels, but a powerful internal drive prevented this. No sooner had he become truly wealthy than he wished to become well known by scholars, and he studied for a few years in Paris (the details of his academic work are unknown). Though he yearned for admiration and approval from professors and fellow students, Schliemann had, in some ways, already surpassed them. During the years, he had taught himself about eight languages, and by 1860 he was equally fluent in English, Russian, German, and French. Turkish probably came last, and it may have been the most difficult. There is no doubt, though, that Schliemann was a real genius, what is called an autodidact, meaning a self-taught person. He may have feared that the burgeoning field of archaeology would pass him by, and there is a discernible haste in his actions, beginning in the 1860s.

Schliemann made his first trip to Asia Minor in the spring of 1867. He knew much about the terrain from his time in the Crimean War, but there were things he could not have known, and there were obstacles that would stand in the way. First and foremost, he had to ask the simple question: Where did Troy lie?

The ancient writers had been almost unanimous on this score. Troy lay just south of the mouth of the Dardanelles. Most of those who read Homer were convinced that Troy was about one to one and a half miles inland, and that the sandy beach, combined with the rugged escarpment above, had been the place where Greeks and Trojans had fought for 10 long terrible years. Schliemann was inclined to trust Homer on all counts, but as he scoured the local area, he could find no significant hillside that close to the open sea. Only when he altered his gaze, looking further inland, did Schliemann find anything that might resemble an archaeological workplace, and even here he was assisted by someone else.

Frank Calvert (1822–1908) has never received the credit he deserves: One might call him the codiscoverer of Troy. A British merchant and a consul for the U.S. government, Calvert had lived for many years in the area near the Dardanelles, and he was convinced that a nearby hillside, which the locals called Hissarlik ("fortified place") held the ruins of Troy. Displaying both energy and will, Calvert purchased part of the hillside from local Turkish farmers and made some tentative digs on the site. Almost from the beginning, he came up with pieces of pottery. Digging deeper, Calvert found the ruins of a Roman temple to the goddess Minerva (synonymous with the Greek goddess Athena). This was almost proof that he was digging on the site that the Romans called Ilium. Calvert was a very careful man, however; he did not wish to ruin anything by digging too far too fast. In this, he was precisely Schliemann's opposite.

ARCHAEOLOGY'S GOLDEN AGE

It is interesting that nineteenth-century archaeologists, who sought to unearth the mysteries of the golden age of Crete, the golden age of Athens, and others themselves participated in a golden age: that of the independent archaeologist.

Archaeology began to move faster in the 1830s, the decade in which a handful of Englishmen and Frenchmen discovered the palaces and throne rooms of the Assyrian Empire in present-day Iraq (the Hittite Empire remained hidden much longer). Schliemann certainly knew of, and may have envied the successes of, these men who unearthed magnificent palace walls, sometimes complete with massive statuary and ornate paintings. Closer to home, he was well aware that Emperor Napoléon III of France (not to be confused with his more famous uncle, Napoléon Bonaparte) had led the way in unearthing the fortress city of Alesia, where Vercingetoriz and the Gauls had resisted Julius Caesar during the Gallic Wars. Schliemann may have feared that he would enter the field too late, that all the great discoveries would soon take place. If he did, that fear was certainly misplaced. Rather, he came to the field just in time, smack in the middle of archaeology's golden age.

SCHLIEMANN AT HISSARLIK

Schliemann and his wife, Sophia, arrived in the winter of 1871. They had cleared permits through the Turkish government in Istanbul, and they were ready for a major attempt at the hill of Hissarlik. Frank Calvert had, by then, become a bystander. There was only room for two people when Schliemann went to work: he and his wife.

In the spring of 1873, Schliemann made considerable progress. He hired about 80 workers—mostly Greeks rather than Turks—and with their shovels and strong backs he excavated a massive trench, starting from the southeast side of Hissarlik. There were days when Schliemann came up with surprising finds, such as inscriptions dating from the Greek city of Ilion, and times when he was empty-handed. There were controversies with Frank Calvert. He and Schliemann had agreed to divide what they found 50–50, and it must be said that Schliemann often fleeced his associate. On at least one occasion, Schliemann persuaded Calvert that a major piece of statuary was worth about one-tenth of its true value.

In April 1873, Sophia Schliemann left the dig site to hasten back to Athens for her father's funeral. For the next two months, Schliemann worked essentially alone, and this happens to be the period in which his biggest finds were made. As his biographer, David A. Traill, points out, Schliemann was a great talent, a man of real genius, but we must not let these talents obscure the less attractive parts of his personality. Two of them emerged on the last day of May 1873.

Schliemann was making rapid progress, and the further that he and the workers dug, the more potential for confusion increased. Not only were priceless pieces of pottery being destroyed in the dig, but Schliemann was slowly coming to the painful conclusion that this might not, *perhaps*, be Homer's Troy after all. So far, he had come upon nothing like the size of the walls and gates as Homer described. It was with great relief, and a sense of his good fortune, that Schliemann came upon "Priam's Gold" on May 31, 1873.

> *I exposed the Trojan circuit wall as it continues from the Scaean Gate and found in one of the rooms of the house of Priam abutting on to this wall a copper container or utensil of the most remarkable shape, about 1 meter long by half a meter broad, for two helmet-like bosses could be seen on it; there was also a bowl with a kind of large candlestick. This*

Sophia Schliemann, wife of Heinrich, won both fame and envy when she posed wearing the "Jewels of Helen" (the royal diadem described in chapter one). After their success at Hissarlik, the Schliemanns went on to excavate at Mycenae, on the Greek mainland.

container was filled with silver and gold vases and cups, which I had to extract, conceal and send away in such haste in order to withdraw them from the greed of my workers *(emphasis added).*

Schliemann said nothing of his *own* greed, of his desire to have Priam's Treasures all to himself. Giving the workers the rest of the morning off, he packed the gold and silver items and laid them aside, so as to be able to send them to Greece and thereby avoid having to share anything with the Turkish government. Making matters even worse, Schliemann lied. He claimed that his wife was with him, that she helped in this moment of concealment, even though every record positively indicates she had gone to Athens and would not return for another 10 days.

Why Schliemann lied remains mysterious. As an archaeologist, one who was setting precedents for a new field of inquiry, it was vital for him to tell the truth and the whole truth concerning each item and every shovelful of earth. Our best surmise is that Schliemann felt some doubt as to whether Hissarlik was indeed Troy (the physical site was so much smaller than Homer's description), and seeing the gold that he immediately attributed to King Priam made him feel both triumphant and fearful. Here was an amazing find, and he could not bear to share it with the Turkish government. More, he felt that this was proof, in some measure, that he had found the true Troy.

The work continued. Schliemann stuck to it all summer and through part of the autumn. His wife had returned, and the two dug ever deeper, coming up against walls, gates, and houses that seemed to suggest that there was more than one Troy underneath. Schliemann knew the slim trail of written evidence as well as any man of his time. He knew that the Greek Ilion had been built on ancient Troy, and that it had been superseded by the Roman Ilium. Even so, he was astonished to find that the layers and levels continued to expand in a vertical sense, and by that autumn Schliemann realized that the place called Hissarlik, which he believed was Troy, had been built on approximately *nine times* during the previous 6,000 years.

The monumental nature of this find cannot be exaggerated. Schliemann went looking for Troy, expecting to find three layers of settlement, and instead he unearthed nine. Much of his work was too hasty—thousands of artifacts had been destroyed in his rapid progress to the bottom—but Schliemann, the self-taught genius, had stumbled upon one of the greatest archaeological finds of all time. In all of the archaeological record before or since, there are probably only about half a dozen places that were settled so many times, and in which the ruins have been uncovered. The *New York Times* commented on Schliemann's work on October 21, 1873:

> *The number of specimens of the most varied character collected amount to fully twenty thousand. The majority of them are made of stone and clay, some of bone, and not a great many of metal. Stone implements are in quantity. There are saws made of flint with teeth carefully cut, and knives of obsidian. There are hammers of stone, with perforations through them to admit of a handle.*

Some of these objects were disappointing to Schliemann at first, because the vast majority were made of stone rather than bronze. But as he pored over his findings, from the safety of his new home in Athens, Schliemann began to realize that his "loss" in finding so little of Bronze Age Troy could also be considered a gain, because he had unearthed so much of Stone Age Troy. The *New York Times* posed the question to its readers in a manner that was fairly flattering to Schliemann:

> *Has Dr. Schliemann driven his explorer's pick through the Homeric Troy, and arrived at even an earlier civilization? Troy, or what remains of it in this nineteenth century, seems to have been but a small place, and the famed citadel but the feudal castle of some petty Prince. Though Troy may be lessened and belittled as to size, should we have found it today still the most glorious of all poems exists, and though stones may molder and vases be ground to dust, the words of the* Iliad *will never perish. Let all praise be given to Dr. Schliemann.*

Schliemann was grateful for the praise, but he wanted more still. He knew that he needed to find more precious objects, and that they needed to reflect the grandeur of the Late Bronze Age in order for him to win the everlasting credit he so desired.

The Face
of Agamemnon

Schliemann had been very fortunate. His excavations at Troy had taken the better part of three summers, rather than the decades that had been spent unearthing the Assyrian ruins. Schliemann was determined not to rest on his laurels, however. If he could not find the broad ax and tower shield of the heroes Ajax or Achilles at Hissarlik, he would go elsewhere in search of them.

MYCENAE

By 1875, archaeology had entered into a new phase. There were still plenty of wealthy amateurs, men who could dig and sift as long as they desired, but the field was also beginning to be populated by professionals, the people who would later form the first academic departments in that subject. Schliemann had brought Troy/Hissarlik to everyone's attention, but he had so claimed the ground there—literally and figuratively—that ambitious young archaeologists tended to look elsewhere. Schliemann himself was looking in a new direction, across the Aegean to the fabled palace of Agamemnon.

In 1876, Schliemann and his wife moved rapidly between Troy/Hissarlik and Athens, looking for a government that would grant them a permit to dig. The Turkish government—now aware that Schliemann had made off with Priam's Gold—was naturally reluctant, and the Schliemanns eventually decided on Mycenae. They arrived there in the summer of 1876 and went straight to work. As at Troy, Schliemann hired a large team of workers, but this time he had to work with a state-sponsored archaeologist: the Greeks were determined not to lose anything valuable from this site.

Numerous scholars had looked at the site of Mycenae previous to Schliemann. The Lion's Gate, a massive sculpture just above the entrance, was still visible from ancient times, and the walls of ruined Mycenae were so thick that modern-day Greeks often claimed that there must have been men like the Cyclops (Cyclopedes) to have built them in the Bronze Age. Schliemann was, again, fortunate, in that few people had ever dug at the site, however, and within a few weeks, his large team of Greek workers had moved thousands of cubic feet of earth. Sophia Schliemann went to Athens for a visit, hoping to win concessions from the Greek government, but its decision stood: the Schliemann couple had to work with the state scientist, who put numerous restrictions on the amount of earth that could be moved. He did not wish to see a repetition of what is now called "Schliemann's Trench" at Troy.

The great breakthrough came in September.

Ever since the time of Homer, Greeks had believed that the tombs of Agamemnon and Cassandra (whom he had taken from Troy) were somewhere at Mycenae. The few archaeologists who had come to look had turned over earth just outside the citadel, however, and Schliemann was the first to set his spade within the fortress. In late November, Schliemann and his workers found a series of grave shafts that seemed to correlate with Homer, and in the next two weeks they unearthed no fewer than five dead persons. Jubilant over his success, Schliemann wrote to a German colleague:

> There are in all 5 tombs, in the smallest of which I found yesterday the bones of a man and a woman covered by at least five kilograms of jewels of pure gold, with the most wonderful archaic, impressed ornaments; even the smallest leaf is covered with them. . . . I have now the firmest conviction that these are the tombs which, as Pausanias, according to the accredited tradition, says belong to Atreus, Agamemnon, Cassandra, Eurymedon, etc. But how different is the civilization which this treasure shows from that of Troy! I write you this in the midst of great turmoil.

Schliemann did not reveal his "turmoil" to anyone at the site, except perhaps his wife. He was distressed by the discrepancy between Mycenaean

THE ILLUSTRATED LONDON NEWS

REGISTERED AT THE GENERAL POST-OFFICE FOR TRANSMISSION ABROAD.

No. 1960.—VOL. LXX.　　SATURDAY, FEBRUARY 3, 1877.　　WITH TWO SUPPLEMENTS | SIXPENCE. By Post, 6½d.

ANTIQUARIAN DISCOVERIES IN GREECE: OUR ARTIST SKETCHING THE ENTRANCE GATE OF THE ACROPOLIS AT MYCENÆ.

A London newspaper's sketch of Schliemann and his wife at Mycenae shows the couple on a dig in search of ancient Grecian treasures. With their Greek counterparts, the Schliemanns discovered the Lion's Gate, a sculpted entryway and the walls of Mycenae.

civilization, as he had unearthed here, and that of Troy, which seemed almost to be in the Stone Age. Typically, Schliemann's enthusiasm did not wane; even in the midst of inner turmoil, he continued to dig, and late in November he came upon the most magnificent tomb of all.

"This corpse [Schliemann wrote] very much resembles the image which my imagination formed long ago of wide-ruling Agamemnon." As is often the case, he was quoted out of context, and the story that reached the newspapers was closer to "I have gazed upon the face of Agamemnon." In either case, Schliemann had indeed achieved something quite wonderful. The gold-masked man he found in the tombs of Mycenae certainly looked as if he might be a king, and by calculating that the man had died at thirty-two or thirty-three, Schliemann made him seem young and energetic enough to have been a "wide-ruling" emperor.

When Schliemann's results were published in *Mycenae* in 1880, his worldwide fame was assured. There were still detractors, to be sure, especially those who criticized his methods of excavation, but it was difficult to argue with the premise that he had done more for archaeology—and knowledge of the ancient world—than any other person of his time. There were still some haunted thoughts, however.

What Schliemann still lacked—and what bothered him intensely—was any direct physical link between the extraordinary palace civilization he had unearthed at Mycenae and the much humbler, almost Stone Age place he had excavated at Troy. Though he felt confident he had gazed "on the face of Agamemnon" and perhaps that of Cassandra, too, Schliemann was worried, disturbed that there was no direct correlation between mainland Greece and the western part of Asia Minor. This drew him back into the field, time and again, and into association with the person that would follow in his footsteps.

Wilhelm Dorpfeld was a German architect, a man with a keen eye for physical space and what might be accomplished with it. About half Schliemann's age, he admired the older man, "the master" as he called him, to the point of adulation. The two first teamed up in the 1880s, and when, in the spring of 1890, they went to Troy/Hissarlik together, they made a significant find. It was not a palace or set of walls, but rather a grand house, located well outside the area Schliemann had dug in the past. There, he and Dorpfeld found a great amount of pottery, and much of it was readily attributed to Mycenean hands. Here, for the first time,

Schliemann had a direct link, clearly establishing that there was a Mycenaean, or early Greek, presence at early Troy. Whether that presence was
warlike, or had been of a mercantile nature, had yet to be seen.

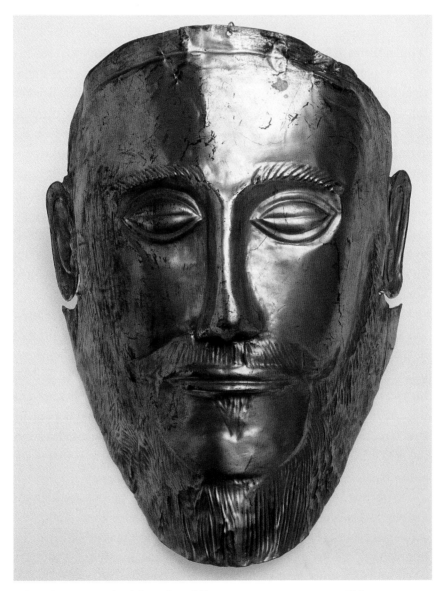

While digging in a burial tomb, Schliemann came across one of his most
important finds: the Mask of Agamemnon. Lifting the beautiful gold mask off
the face of an entombed body, Schliemann believed that he had found the
tomb of the famous Agamemnon, king of Mycenae.

Most of the people who study Schliemann believe that the old man (as they call him) was worn out and full of regret. Very likely, he realized that his immense digging in 1873 (Schliemann's Trench) had obliterated thousands of objects and moved from their original site, making the archaeological task more difficult. Not only this, but Schliemann felt the press of his years—he had been traveling and working almost nonstop for decades. He confided to his journal that "it is not too late," meaning that he could still find some other tie-in, something else to connect the Stone Age city he had found with the Bronze Age of Homer. But it was too late.

Schliemann died in Naples, Italy, on December 26, 1890. Family and friends were close to him at the end, and his body was taken to Athens for burial: He and his wife, Sophia (who outlived him by many years), are both buried in the First Cemetery of Athens. At the time of his death, Schliemann was still the "grand old man" of Western archaeology; his name and deeds were venerated by scholars and laymen alike. He would only hold that position for another decade, however, and his critics would increase as the years passed.

DORPFELD AT TROY

Determined to finish what the old man had begun, Wilhelm Dorpfeld started his own series of excavations. He was funded, in part, by Sophia Schliemann and by Kaiser Wilhelm II of Germany.

Dorpfeld did not have Schliemann's precise eye for pieces of pottery, knives, or the like, but he had an excellent architect's vision of what Troy had been like. In the spring of 1890, Dorpfeld and Schliemann, together, had dug well outside the walls of the main citadel, and Dorpfeld continued on this track. His work commenced in 1893; that year, he discovered a set of outlying walls that Schliemann had missed entirely. It was never Dorpfeld's way to upstage or to contradict "the master," but his work soon established that Troy was bigger than the small citadel Schliemann had found. Coming upon walls that were about 30 feet high and extremely well made of dressed limestone blocks, Dorpfeld expanded his vision. If Troy was not as large as Homer had described, it was certainly larger than the small citadel on the top of Hissarlik.

Working with the classical texts, Dorpfeld found some correlations between Homer and the outlying walls. Homer had described, very particularly, how Patroclus had three times failed to scale Troy's angled walls, and Dorpfeld produced photographs that showed the world that the outlying walls did indeed have a curious, outward slant that made it difficult for them to be surmounted. As the nineteenth century neared its end, Dorpfeld prepared a massive archaeological work, a book in German which, unfortunately, was never translated into English. He had gone beyond the master, yet he had mostly confirmed the master as correct. Dorpfeld was upstaged, however, at that very moment by another heroic archaeologist, one cast in the nature of Schliemann.

SIR ARTHUR EVANS

Arthur Evans was born in England in 1851 to a middle-class family that had recently achieved great success in the paper mill industry. Given more leisure time than the average Victorian—and a lengthy stay at Oxford—Evans committed himself to the life of the mind. Shortly after the death

THE NEW GREAT WAR

Every generation speaks of a time of great trial, often connected to war. For Homer and his listeners, the Trojan War was the great national epic, the event that bound them together as victorious Greeks. For Virgil, the Trojan War was the beginning of Rome's glory, for from the ashes of Troy fled Aeneas and his followers, who became the ancestors of Julius Caesar and the men and women of Virgil's time, the first century B.C. But to men and women of the early twentieth century, the Great War was surely what we now call the First World War or World War I.

The First World War began in 1914, pitting the Allied Powers of Britain, France, Russia, and their allies against the Central Powers of Germany, Austria-Hungary, and the Ottoman Turkish Empire. It is the last of these powers—Turkey—that made a connection between the Trojan War of 1275 B.C. and World War I.

In 1915, Britain sent a vast fleet of ships—practically an armada—to capture Istanbul, capital of the Ottoman Empire. The British, Australian, and New Zealander troops found that the Dardanelles was too of his wife in 1893, Evans came across a handful of "incised seal stones," which seemed to indicate that the ancient Minoans—the people of Crete—had indeed possessed a form of writing. The lack of anything like this had been a serious stumbling block for Schliemann, who found it difficult to believe that the civilized and powerful Mycenaeans of Homer's time were not literate.

Following his initial hunch, Arthur Evans began a series of excavations on Crete in the spring of 1900 (just as Dorpfeld's book was going to press), and it is no exaggeration to say that his finds were among the most remarkable of all time, second only to Schliemann in many people's opinion. Going only a few feet deep, Evans found a throne room, a series of apartments, and a series of frescoes that can only be described as stunning; the women captured in these paintings and the male athletes jumping over bulls have no parallel in Western archaeology. These were

packed with Turkish mines, so the men were landed on the peninsula of Gallipoli, right across the Dardanelles from Hissarlik/Troy. The irony was not lost on the Allied soldiers, many of whom had read Homer.

The Gallipoli campaign was one of the worst of the entire war, from the Allied point of view. About 200,000 Allied soldiers went killed, wounded, or missing, and the Turks may have lost even more. From the Turkish view, however, the fight for Gallipoli was a smashing success: They turned back the Allied invaders. And, even as the fighting in far-off Belgium led to poetry about "Flanders' Field," so did the war on Gallipoli lead to allegories and comparisons between the Trojans and Greeks of the second millennium B.C. with the British, Australian, and New Zealanders of the twentieth century. One can certainly ask if humans have progressed much since the Late Bronze Age. One can even ponder whether the weapons of modern war—the tank, machine gun, and grenade—are but technical improvements on the destructive weapons of Homer's time: the sword, shield, and rock sling.

Arthur Evans, an Englishman, began digging in Crete in the early twentieth century and discovered a wealth of artifacts that rivaled Schliemann's finds. One of his most impressive discoveries was a richly decorated throne room that featured beautiful frescoes and paintings. A restored view is shown here.

remarkable enough, but Evans also found many clay-baked tablets, which clearly showed that the Minoans of the fourteenth and fifteenth centuries B.C. were literate. Their scribes had been conscientious record keepers, and the Minoan civilization (Evans named it for the legendary King Minos) had some of the world's oldest writing.

Evans was a great genius, like Schliemann, but like the "old man," he also had his blind spots. From the very beginning, Evans insisted that the Minoan civilization had taken precedence over the mainland Greek one and that the ruins Schliemann had unearthed at Mycenae could only have been colonies of the island civilization of Crete. Many people did not agree with this thesis, but Evans rose to become such a towering figure in the world of archaeology that it was difficult, perhaps dangerous, to disagree with him. Dorpfeld's work at Troy was almost completely forgotten, and Western scholars spoke of the Minoan civilization and its grandeurs, assigning Mycenae to a poorly rated second, and Troy/Hissarlik to a very distant third.

That still left the Hittites, however. Excavations of the former Hittite Empire came a generation after the great discoveries at Troy/Hissarlik and Mycenae. The Hittites had been so "lost" that no one knew who was meant by the "king of Hatti," often mentioned in letters from the Egyptian diplomatic corps. That situation changed in 1906 when Hittite cities were discovered in what is now Bocazcoy, Turkey. Excavation of the capital city took many years, but the labors of the German archaeologists proved—beyond the shadow of a doubt—that the Hittite Empire had been very grand, operating as an equal of the Egyptian or Babylonian ones of the time.

By the time another great war broke out—this one between the Central Powers and the Allied ones—the historians and archaeologists knew a great deal more about the ancient past.

Scientific Teams

The age of the romantic genius came to a close in the early twentieth century. It is well known that a group of archaeologists found King Tutankhamen's tomb in 1922, but that was one of the last great finds by an independent group. The age of the trained scientist, whose loyalty was to a specific university, had arrived.

CARL BLEGEN

He was born in Minneapolis, Minnesota, in 1887. Inspired by his father, who was an academic, Blegen earned degrees from Augsburg Seminary, the University of Minnesota, and Yale University. By the time he went to Greece in 1910, he was a confirmed lover of all things Greek. Intrigued by the Bronze Age, Blegen did his first archaeological digs at Korakou, Greece. He became a specialist both in determining the age of Mediterranean pottery and in using soil samples—sedimentary levels—to determine the age of a place.

In 1927, he began teaching at the University of Cincinnati, where he was an inspired and inspiring lecturer. Like many of his generation, Blegen was eager to have archaeology lose the "devil-may-care" reputation it had earned in the days of Heinrich Schliemann. At the same time, Blegen was a quiet romantic, treasuring Homer and Virgil almost as much as soil samples and Mycenaean pottery.

The beginning of the 1930s—when the United States and much of Europe was mired in the Great Depression—does not seem like an opportune time for archaeology, but Blegen persuaded the University of

Cincinnati to fund a major set of digs at Troy. Not only was this a genuine scientific team, with rules of evidence and professional conduct established in advance, but Blegen's team was also the first to have moving pictures (motion photography) on the scene.

Blegen's excavation of Troy/Hissarlik was the third, after Schliemann's and Dorpfeld's. Schliemann had established that at least four cities had existed on this spot, and Dorpfeld had shown that the outer city walls were much larger and grander than previously believed. Both men had operated on slim budgets and without the presence of academic supervision: It was different with Blegen.

Beginning in the summer of 1932, and continuing to 1938, Blegen slowly established that there had been even more occupants of Troy/Hissarlik than previously thought. No fewer than nine levels of cities existed, Blegen said, and some of them had subdivisions, leading to assigned titles such as Troy VI Aa or Troy VII B. Blegen's first, very substantial achievement was to demonstrate that one of these levels, Troy VII A, had been ruined by fire. There was no specific evidence of warfare, however, and Blegen began to consider the possibility that this had been a natural—not human-made—catastrophe. This was heresy so far as the purist readers of Homer were concerned, and Blegen earns credit as the first truly professional archaeologist of Troy, a person who would go exactly where the evidence took him and no further. Blegen did fall victim to a series of hypotheses, however.

Coming across a storeroom and a bakery, Blegen began to hypothesize about a state of siege, a place where the defenders of Troy secured their bread and wine. He was careful to use precise academic terms in describing the situation, but enthusiastic Homerists read between the lines. The longer Blegen dug, the more convinced he was that Troy/Hissarlik held many more secrets, and that making the links between Stone Age Troy, Bronze Age Troy, and the Greek and Roman cities of Ilion and Ilium could supply answers to the questions of ancient history. Toward the end of his six summers of excavation, Blegen came across a remarkable find, an arrowhead that he said was clearly of eastern Mediterranean make. The arrowhead (still possessed by the University of Cincinnati) became almost an article of faith for those who believed that Hissarlik and Troy were precisely synonymous. Blegen was much more careful, using the evidence to show what it could, but years later, when he wrote *Troy and the Trojans*, he said that there was no doubt in his mind that this, Hissarlik, was indeed the Troy of Achilles and Agamemnon, Priam and Paris.

Blegen was not finished, however.

PYLOS

In the summer of 1939, just before the Second World War began, Blegen transferred his attention to mainland Greece. He knew that the tablets uncovered at Knossos were still undecipherable, and he wanted to settle one of the long-standing questions: Did the Mycenaeans speak Greek? Or some other language? Neither the ruins at Mycenae nor those at Tiryns had provided an answer.

Earlier, we employed Homer to see that Telemachus—the son of Odysseus—had gone in search of his father. Telemachus had visited Menelaus and Helen in Sparta, but even before that, he had seen old King

"WOMEN OF ASIA"

In the opening chapter, we heard Helen (through the voice of Homer) lament about the loss of the "lovely comradeship of women my own age." Later, in Chapter 3, we saw that aristocratic women like Helen did exist, and that their lives were as occupied with merriment as with labor (harvesting saffron). What about the women captives of Troy, however, those that King Nestor spoke of, the "slave women in their low hip girdles?"

They came to light in the Pylos archive, discovered in 1939. The clay tablets—which had been hard baked in a fire—show all sorts of documentary links that had previously not existed. For example, we now know that there were about 1,500 slave women at Pylos, harvesting flax to be made into linen, and that many of them were indeed labeled "women of Asia." This is not proof that the Trojan War took place as Homer describes it, but it lends plausibility to the idea. If Helen's beauty was such that her face launched 1,000 ships, bringing on the Trojan War, then the much sought-after women of Asia may have been another reason why the Greeks crossed the Aegean Sea to attack Troy.

Nestor at "sandy Pylos." Because there was a twentieth-century town of that name, and because some ruins had been unearthed, Carl Blegen went there in the summer of 1939. After speaking with the locals and looking for sites that corresponded to Homer, Blegen stumbled upon one of the greatest finds in archaeological history. Within hours of beginning to dig, he and his team came across hundreds of stone and clay tablets, written in a form of language clearly different from those found at Knossos in 1900. The importance of the find cannot be overestimated. Until Blegen found "sandy Pylos," many historians had been content to believe that the Minoan civilization had been literate and, presumably, advanced but that the Mycenaean had been backward.

The clay tablets could not be deciphered immediately. About 12 years after Blegen's astonishing discovery at Pylos, a young Englishman—with little formal training in linguistics—managed to "crack" the code of Linear B, as it is now known. From his work, modern historians are confident that the Myceaneans and the people of Pylos were literate and that it is possible that they, not the people of Crete, were the overlords of the Aegean world in the Late Bronze Age.

THE GREAT GAP

Archaeology had to pause during the Second World War. Not only was little work accomplished, but science was set back—in some ways—by the destruction caused by the war. The British Museum in London was spared any significant bombing during the "Blitz" launched by Hitler's airplanes, but the same cannot be said in reverse. Hundreds of British and American bombers flew over the major German cities each day, dropping bombs that destroyed lives, to be certain, but also sometimes landed on priceless artifacts, whether in museums or elsewhere.

In the winter of 1945, as the war approached its end, the Soviet Union made a major drive for Berlin. The Russians wanted to take the German capital as revenge for the many atrocities committed against their civilians during the four-year war on the Eastern Front. As the Russians came closer, and as they entered the city itself, leading German scientists did their best to hide or spirit to safety priceless artifacts. One set of these was the Treasures of Priam, unearthed by Heinrich Schliemann in 1873.

Schliemann had donated the Treasures of Priam to the Berlin Museum, where they had been used, sometimes by Hitler, as a propaganda piece for the glories of German civilization. As the Russians approached, the silver,

Based on his past research and stories from the *Odyssey* of Telemachus visiting King Nestor's home, archaeologist Carl Blegen began searching for ancient artifacts in Pylos. Blegen used classic texts and information from the locals to determine the location of the king's palace, where he found many indecipherable clay and stone tablets. Above, the hearth of Nestor's palace in Pylos, shown here.

gold, and jewels were boxed, but before they could be taken away, the Russians took the building and the city. Given that millions of Germans were dead at the end of the war, and that millions of others were homeless or displaced, it took some time before a postwar international committee began to ask what had happened to archaeological treasures from all over Western Europe. The answer is that Hitler and the top Nazis had coveted such materials, taking them from places like Paris and Krakow and hoarding them (Hitler's second-in-command, Hermann Goering, had a huge, priceless art collection all to himself).

The committees set up after the war could only say that the Treasures of Priam had disappeared. No one would admit to having taken them.

Beyond doubt, the treasures had been taken by Russian soldiers, but there was no way to investigate what went on behind the Iron Curtain that descended over the Soviet Union in 1947. Whatever the Russians had, or did not have, they were not saying.

Archaeologists had to pick up from the rubble and the ruins. Many of them lamented what had happened to their science, saying that the glorious days of Heinrich Schliemann, Sir Arthur Evans, and Carl Blegen were gone forever. In some ways they were correct. But the relatively new science of archaeology strangely benefited in some ways, and a new crop of scholars— mostly sent by universities—would pick up where the individual geniuses left off.

BLEGEN'S FINAL WORD

Carl Blegen's *Troy and the Trojans* was published by Praeger Publishers in 1963. Even those who considered Blegen a careful, cautious scholar remarked that the twentieth-century master of Troy's archaeology had taken a very long time to write his master work. When they turned the 172 pages and saw the 67 photographs, they were convinced, however. This was a real masterpiece, one that only someone involved with Troy for more than 20 years could write. On page 20, Blegen stated his major interpretation of his many findings:

> *It can no longer be doubted, when one surveys the state of our knowledge today, that there really was an actual historical Trojan War in which a coalition of Achaeans, or Mycenaeans, under a king whose overlordship was recognized, fought against the people of Troy and*

After more than 20 years of research, Carl Blegen published his findings on Troy in 1963. Those who had previously doubted the existence of Troy were able to see images of the unearthed Trojan ruins (*above*) and the artifacts that were discovered at the site.

their allies. The magnitude and the duration of the struggle may have been exaggerated by folk memory in later times, and the numbers of the participants have been very over-generously estimated in the epic poems.

Still, Blegen was convinced that the Trojan War did take place and that the hill of Hissarlik was indeed the place besieged by the early Greeks. That was enough for many people, and quite a few specialists declared that Blegen had done all the really important work. There was little more to do at Troy/Hissarlik, they said.

As so often, the experts were mistaken.

Troy in
Our Time

We're dealing with a myth, whether we want to or not.
—Manfred Korfmann, 2004

One might think that the horrors of twentieth-century warfare—including
the appearance of the tank, machine gun, and the atomic bomb—would
reduce the interest of contemporary peoples in Troy and the Trojan War.
One might believe that people would be weary of war and select only
peaceful places for their archaeological investigations. This is not the case,
however. If anything, the terrible calamities of World War I and World
War II persuaded many people—scholars and laymen alike—to show a
renewed interest in the classical world of Greece and Rome, and the mysteries that lay even further back: the time of Troy.

NINE CITIES

In 1963, Carl Blegen's final work was published. *Troy and the Trojans* was a
masterpiece of scientific investigation, and Blegen made it clear that Troy
had been built at least nine different times (whether it had the same name
each time is debatable). Blegen went slowly, carefully going through the
investigations of Schliemann and Dorpfeld, explaining what these men
had seen and what they had failed to see. Blegen never touted himself as
the end-all authority, but his description and analysis of the nine superim-
posed layers of settlement established him as the greatest Trojan scholar
of his time. In his opinion, Troy VI A, as he called it, was the Troy of the
time of Priam, Hector, and Paris.

Blegen's work could have been the final word, but a renewed interest in archaeology pushed the investigations further. Carbon-14 dating had been developed in the year 1950, and scholars of the 1970s and 1980s had means of measurement that had never previously been available. At the same time, Homer's work entered yet another renaissance, or rebirth. A classic translation of the *Odyssey* was accomplished by Robert Fitzgerald in 1960; it was followed by other translations of the *Iliad*, and by about 1980, one could say that more people were reading Homer than ever before. Troy and its people also benefited—at a great distance over time—from an interdisciplinary approach to classical studies. Recent archaeological digs in Egypt, Crete, and above all Turkey, which had formerly been known as Asia Minor, revealed that the Trojans lived at an especially rich time in the Late Bronze Age. There had been flourishing "palace" civilizations on Crete and mainland Greece, and the Hittites reached the height of their power in the thirteenth century B.C.

New methods of investigation were joined by renewed interest, and the work at Troy continued.

MICHAEL WOOD

In 1985, the British Broadcasting Corporation (BBC) brought out one of the most ambitious descriptions of scientific work ever displayed on the television screen. Writer and director Michael Wood was given about six hours to lay out *In Search of the Trojan War*, and no one ever did it better for a general audience. Tall, lean, and endlessly enthusiastic, Wood traveled to all the major sites—Troy, Mycenae, Pylos, Knossos—and explained to the viewer what was known and what was not. There, on-screen for the first time, the viewer could see the hard-baked tablets that contained Linear A (still not deciphered) and Linear B (known and understood by scholars). Wood was one of the first Troy popularizers to emphasize the importance of the Hittites, who, after all, had controlled much of Asia Minor during the time of the Trojan War. There are, as Wood showed, some intriguing references to a place that the Hittites called Wilusa, and a handful of others—passed down to us by the Hittite royal bureaucrats—of a mysterious kingdom called Alahawia.

Was Wilusa Troy? Was Alahawia Mycenae?

No one could be certain. Even as he laid out the tangibles and intangibles, Michael Wood led the viewer to something else: the lost Treasures

Blegen's unearthed stone and clay tablets were finally deciphered 12 years after they were discovered in Pylos. Known as Linear B, the language carved into these tablets revealed a great deal about Mycenaean civilization and its dominance in the region.

of Priam. In the film, Wood went to the Berlin Museum to speak with curators. The television film showed replicas that had been made of the Priam Treasures, but the originals had, of course, been missing since April 1945, when the Russian army entered Berlin.

By the end of the 1980s, Michael Wood's brilliant telecast seemed as if it was the final word on Troy. If it raised as many questions as it answered, the same could be said for almost all previous attempts. What Wood had done, though, was present the material in such a way that Troy and the Trojan War again became household words, and the interested layperson could discuss the many theories about Troy almost as well as the informed specialist.

As so often in the case of Troy, a surprise caught almost everyone unawares.

PRIAM'S TREASURES

The Soviet Union dissolved in 1991 and was replaced by the new Russian Federation. Pressure built on Russian scholars to open their archives to Western ones, and in 1994 it was announced that the Treasures of Priam had been found, rusting away in the cellar of one of Russia's great museums. Precisely how the Treasures of Priam had left Berlin and made their way to St. Petersburg was not fully described; the important thing is that dozens of Western specialists were able to examine the treasures in 1994. They reported that what they had expected—from Schliemann's notes and from the replicas in the Berlin Museum—agreed very much with what they found. King Priam's Treasures existed. The gold diadems were there, much as Schliemann had described. The masks and funeral objects remained, as well. The precise worth of the objects could not be determined, but for scholars who wanted a look at Bronze Age Troy, they were simply priceless. One great mystery had been partially solved. Others still remained.

KORFMANN

Manfred Korfmann became the fourth great archaeologist of Troy. Schliemann had been the first, followed by his student Dorpfeld, then thirty years had passed before Carl Blegen took up the work. Many years passed before Korfmann and a team of archaeologists from the University of Tubingen took up the mantle, but by the 1990s, their work was in full swing.

Korfmann and his team possessed advantages over earlier groups. They had carbon dating, and they had much more time to dig slowly and analyze what they found. Perhaps most important, they were able to compare their finds with those from other archaeological digs in Egypt, Turkey, and Greece.

By the late 1990s, Korfmann and his team had clearly established that Bronze Age Troy, especially Level VI A, was much bigger than previously believed. Just as Dorpfeld had found walls that Schliemann had missed, Korfmann and his group expanded further south of the citadel, revealing that Troy VI A was about *fifteen times bigger* than previously assumed. It was still not as large as Knossos or Mycenae, but for the first time one could argue that Troy VI A had a population of between 6,000 and 7,000.

TROY IN FILM

Homeric legends have been popular with screenwriters and directors for decades, but it was only in 2004 that one of them was presented in a full-blown motion picture epic. This was Wolfgang Petersen's *Troy*, released in the spring of that year.

Petersen already possessed a fine reputation. German by birth, he had directed the blockbuster *Das Boot*, a film about German U-boat men in World War II, in 1980. He had bettered this with *The Perfect Storm*, his film about Massachusetts fishermen, released in 2000. Petersen's most ambitious work was *Troy*, however; for this, he had a cast of hundreds, and computer-generated men and women in the thousands. The film begins with a set piece of Achilles' amazing prowess, a scene that is not mentioned in the *Iliad*.

Achilles (played by Brad Pitt) is called upon, as King Agamemnon's champion, to fight an enormous 7-foot-tall man put up by the king of the Thracians. Achilles dons his armor and round shield (not the tower shields depicted on Mycenaean pottery) to charge the much bigger man, who, surprised, hurls his spear. Dodging the spear, Achilles comes close, suddenly leaps about 4 feet off the ground, and comes down to sink his sword into the man's neck. The "fight" has lasted about 10 seconds, and Achilles is the undisputed champion.

Admittedly, this still did not come up to the level of Homeric poetry, where 100,000 Greeks had besieged many thousands of Trojans.

Korfmann and his group were frustrated, however, by something that had also plagued all the earlier Troy archaeologists: the absence of writing. The closest they found was an inscribed stone. Just as one arrowhead does not a war make, so the discovery of one piece of symbolic writing does not indicate a truly literate culture. But the more that Korfmann and his team investigated, the more they came to associate Troy as Wilusa, and a vassal state of the Hittites.

This, as numerous scholars declare, is the key to discovering more about Troy.

This powerful scene—which ends with the Thracians meekly surrendering their land to Agamemnon—sets the stage for what is essentially a war of champions between Achilles and Hector, Paris and Menelaus.

Other, less violent scenes involve King Priam (played by the legendary Peter O'Toole), Helen (portrayed by Diane Kruger), and other Trojans. Most impressive is the reconstruction of the walls and battlements of Troy. Seeing them, and the desperate attacks the Greeks make, the viewer can be forgiven for believing that Wolfgang Petersen has brought the Bronze Age to life. Of course, there are discrepancies and things that seem to miss their mark. One of the most poignant is that the beach on which most of the action is filmed faces in the wrong direction, so that the sun rises from the opposite location from what is expected. Another is that the director makes almost no use of the common man or woman. Troy, or the Troy of 2004, is almost exclusively about the elite, Trojan and Greek alike.

With all the things it misses, *Troy* is clearly the most ambitious and, to date, the most successful portrayal of a Bronze Age historic situation. Whether future filmmakers will attempt to build on this success or leave it to stand alone remains unknown.

EASTERN SOURCES

From Heinrich Schliemann's time to the present, the emphasis has always been on discovering connections between Troy on the Dardanelles and the Mycenaean/Greek world 400 miles to the west. Schliemann's discoveries at Mycenae and Tiryns and Carl Blegen's at Pylos have been instrumental in our understanding of the Late Bronze Age Greeks. They have turned up so little connection with Troy, however, that it is time to incorporate the body of knowledge that exists from about 500 miles to the east.

Much more is known of the Hittites than ever before. Their writing script was deciphered about 1915, and the discoveries since have been rather remarkable. We know today, for example, that the Hittite Empire was nearly as great as the Egyptian and that the two peoples clashed several times, with each seeking dominance in the lands in-between. But the Hittites were brought to their knees in the twelfth century B.C., and something similar also happened to the Egyptians. In both cases, the culprits are a little-known group, or amalgam, called the Sea Peoples.

Just who the Sea Peoples were remains subject to debate. The only ethnic group that can be positively identified as a Sea People is the Philistines mentioned in the Egyptian tablets, who then retreated to present-day Israel. Other than that, the Sea Peoples are a gray, amorphous group, but scholars increasingly lean to the belief that they were made up of Greeks, Cypriots, peoples from Asia Minor, and others. In other words, they were too widespread and too many to be identified.

Whatever their ethnic backgrounds, the Sea Peoples brought the Late Bronze Age to a stunning, sharp end, sometime in the twelfth century B.C. Egypt survived in a weakened state; the Mycenaean civilization practically disappeared, as did the Hittites. So how did Troy fare?

All we can say for certain is that Troy was rebuilt. The city on the mound that we now call Hissarlik was built as early as 3000 B.C., and then rebuilt eight times over the centuries. Clearly, this was a place that invited invaders—or suffered from natural disasters—and one that practically begged to be rebuilt, time and again.

The wheel has come around through 3,200 years, and we pose the same questions that we heard in the opening chapter.

Was Helen truly that beautiful? Very likely yes. She was not the main cause of the Trojan War, however; commercial motivations ranked much higher than the abduction of one, or even a number, of women.

The ruins of Troy can be viewed in its original location, near the Aegean Sea and the Dardanelles. Located in modern-day Hissarlik, Turkey, ancient Troy is forever linked to myth, romance, and heroism.

Did the Greeks send 1,000 ships to bring her home? Almost certainly not. There were, most likely, not 1,000 ships in all of Greece at the time, and most of them would have been needed for fishing, one of the mainstays of the Greek economy.

Were the towers of Troy as high as Homer describes? Definitely not. The city of Troy—situated on the mound we call Hissarlik—was a substantial place of between 6,000 and 7,000 souls, but the towers that Homer describes are something from the poetic imagination. Homer, of course, lived 400 years after the events. That still leaves the final, most important question: What can the lives and deaths of Late Bronze Age peoples tell us about ourselves, their descendants?

If we read Homer closely, we see that men and women suffered from similar anxieties and thrilled to similar triumphs to what we experience today. This is why Homer remains so important, 2,800 years after he sang his epics.

The chances are that Homer, the *Iliad*, and the *Odyssey* will continue to be central to the Western canon for centuries to come. Neither we nor our descendants will forget Achilles, Agamemnon, or Hector, all of whom contribute to our view of the perfections and limitations of men. Nor will Helen, Cassandra, and Andromache be forgotten: Women of the future will read their stories and—we expect—both laugh and weep. Therefore, when one asks, "Is Homer still important to us today?" the answer must be in the affirmative.

Chronology

c. 3000 B.C.	Troy first settled
c. 2200 B.C.	Destruction of Troy II
1600–1150 B.C.	Late Bronze Age
1275 B.C.	Likely time for Trojan-Greek War
1250–1150 B.C.	Invasions of the Sea Peoples
c. 1175	Hittite Empire collapses
1150–750 B.C.	Greek Dark Age
8th century B.C.	Lifetime of Homer
7th century B.C.	Greek alphabet emerges
6th century B.C.	The *Iliad* and the *Odyssey* committed to writing
480 B.C.	Xerxes, king of kings, sacrifices bulls at Troy
336 B.C.	Alexander the Great comes to Troy
51 B.C.	Julius Caesar comes to Troy
40–30 B.C.	Virgil composes the *Aeneid*
29 B.C.	Augustus Caesar comes to Troy
A.D. 350	Roman town of Ilium mentioned
1715	Alexander Pope translates the *Iliad*
1871	Heinrich Schliemann arrives at Hissarlik
1873	Schliemann finds the Treasures of Priam
1876	Schliemann excavates at Mycenae, finds tombs
1893–1894	Wilhelm Dorpfeld excavates at Troy
1900	Arthur Evans excavates at Knossos on Crete
1900–1915	Major Hittite cities excavated by German teams
1922	Tomb of King Tut opened
1932–1938	Carl Blegen excavates at Troy
1939	Blegen excavates at Pylos

1945	Treasures of Priam disappear at end of World War II
1963	*Troy and the Trojans* published in New York
1993	Manfred Korfmann excavates at Troy

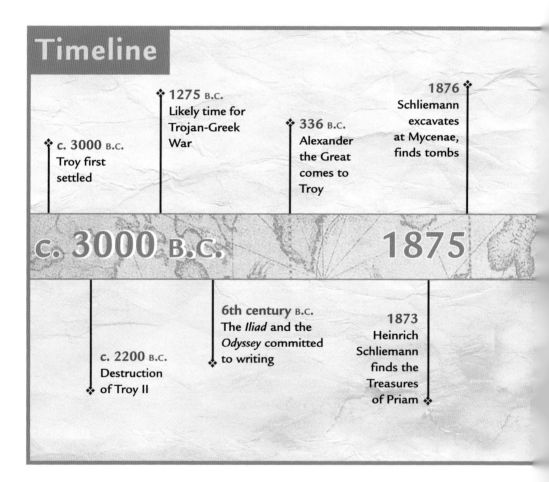

Timeline

❖ **c. 3000** B.C.
Troy first
settled

❖ **1275** B.C.
Likely time for
Trojan-Greek
War

❖ **336** B.C.
Alexander
the Great
comes to
Troy

1876 ❖
Schliemann
excavates
at Mycenae,
finds tombs

C. 3000 B.C.   1875

c. 2200 B.C.
Destruction
❖ of Troy II

6th century B.C.
The *Iliad* and the
Odyssey committed
❖ to writing

1873
Heinrich
Schliemann
finds the
Treasures
of Priam ❖

1994	Treasures of Priam found in St. Petersburg, Russia
2004	*Troy* released to the cinema
2005	Manfred Korfmann dies in Germany

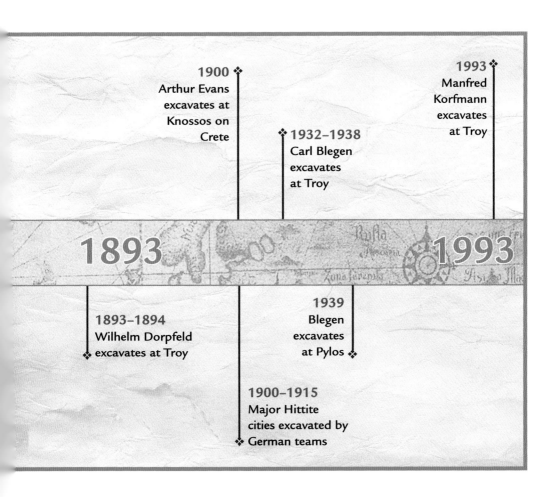

Glossary

Achilles   A major protagonist in Homer's *Iliad*.

Aegean Sea   Body of water between Turkey and Greece.

Agamemnon   King of the Greeks in Homer's *Iliad*.

Anatolia   Ancient name for what is now Turkey (sometimes called Asia Minor).

Bosporus   Narrow body of water that connects the Sea of Marmara to the Black Sea. Modern city of Istanbul straddles the Bosporus.

Dardanelles/Hellespont   Narrow body of water that connects the Aegean Sea to the Sea of Marmara. Troy/Hissarlik lies within five miles.

diadem   A jeweled crown.

Hector   Trojan prince who defends his city in Homer's *Iliad*.

Helen   Spartan queen whose abduction by Prince Paris brings on the Trojan War.

Hissarlik   Place in Turkey that Schliemann excavated in the 1870s.

Hittites   People who dominated Anatolia (Turkey) in the second millennium B.C.

Homer   Blind poet who sang the *Iliad* and the *Odyssey* about 400 years after the events took place.

Homeric   The highest praise that can be given to a piece of literature.

Marmara   Large inland sea that lies between the Hellespont and the Bosporus.

Menelaus   Spartan king who mobilizes the Greeks to regain Helen.

Minoan   A civilization on the island of Crete, named for the legendary King Minos.

Mycenaean   Civilization on mainland Greece that flourished in the second millennium B.C.

Odysseus   King of Ithaca, island on west coast of Greece. Protagonist of the *Odyssey*, sung by the poet Homer.

Paris   Trojan prince who abducts Queen Helen of Sparta.

Priam   King of Troy; father of Hector and Paris.

Priam's Treasures   Jewels discovered by Heinrich Schliemann, brought to Germany, and then taken to Russia at the end of World War II.

Sea Peoples   Nomadic invaders who attacked areas throughout the eastern Mediterranean, bringing the Late Bronze Age to an end.

Trojan War   A 10-year siege, described by Homer in the *Iliad.*

Troy   Perhaps the most fabled name in world history, owing to the magnificent storytelling of Homer.

Bibliography

Bauer, Susan Wise. *The History of the Ancient World: From the Earliest Accounts to the Fall of Rome*. New York: W.W. Norton, 2007.

Drews, Robert. *The End of the Bronze Age: Changes in Warfare and the Catastrophe CA. 1200 B.C.* Princeton, N.J.: Princeton University Press, 1993.

Fox, Robin Lane. *Traveling Heroes in the Epic Age of Homer*. New York: Random House, 2008.

Freely, John. *Children of Achilles: The Greeks in Asia Minor Since the Days of Troy*. London: I.B. Tauris, 2010.

Homer. *The Iliad*, trans. Robert Fagles. New York: Penguin Books, 1990.

Homer. *The Odyssey*, trans. Robert Fitzgerald. New York: Farrar, Straus and Giroux, 1998.

Hughes, Bettany. *Helen of Troy: The Story Behind the Most Beautiful Woman in the World*. New York: Random House, 2005.

Moorehead, Caroline. *Lost and Found: The 9,000 Treasures of Troy*. New York: Viking Penguin, 1996.

Ryan, William, and Walter Pitman. *Noah's Flood: The New Scientific Discoveries About the Event That Changed History*. New York: Simon and Schuster, 1998.

Toltsikov, Vladimir, and Mikhail Treister. *The Gold of Troy: Searching for Homer's Fabled City*, translated from the Russian by Christina Sever and Mila Bonnischen. New York: Harry N. Abrams, 1996.

Traill, David A. *Schliemann of Troy: Treasure and Deceit*. New York: St. Martin's Press, 1995.

Virgil, *The Aeneid*, trans. Robert Fagles. New York: Penguin Books, 2006.

Winkler, Martin M., ed. *Troy: From Homer's Iliad to Hollywood Epic*. Malden, Mass.: Blackwell Publishing, 2007.

Wood, Michael. *In Search of the Trojan War*. London: BBC, 1985.

Further Resources

Hawaas, Zahi. "Tut's Family Secrets: DNA Sheds New Light on the Boy King's Life and Death." *National Geographic*, September 2010: pp. 34–55.

Korfmann, Manfred. *Troy: Battlefield of Myth and Truth*. Princeton, N.J.: Films for the Humanities and Sciences, 2004.

Martin, Thomas R. *Ancient Greece: From Prehistoric to Hellenistic Times*. New Haven, Conn.: Yale University Press, 1996.

Strauss, Barry. *The Trojan War: A New History*. New York: Simon and Schuster, 2006.

Thorndike, Joseph J., ed. *Mysteries of the Past*. New York: American Heritage, 1971.

Web Sites

Project Troia
http://www.uni-tuebingen.de/troy/eng/sttroica.html

Troy—University of Cincinnati
http://www.cerhas.uc.edu/troy
University Web site that provides many angles of the story of Troy, especially those connected with the digs of Carl Blegen and Manfred Korfmann.

Archaeological Site of Troy (UNESCO)
http://whc.unesco.org
Troy became a UNESCO World Heritage Site in 1998.

Picture Credits

Index

About the Author

SAMUEL WILLARD CROMPTON is a historian and biographer who lives in the Pioneer Valley of western Massachusetts. Like many Americans growing up in the 1970s, he was entranced with stories of archaeology; the finds of that time seemed to rival those of the 1870s. Crompton teaches history at Holyoke Community College. He is the author or editor of many books, including *Alexander the Great* and *Julius Caesar*, both written for Chelsea House.